99 FAVORITE AMISH Soups & Stews

GEORGIA VAROZZA

HARVEST HOUSE PUBLISHERS
EUGENE, OREGON

Cover by Dugan Design Group

Cover photo © Dugan Design Group

99 FAVORITE AMISH SOUPS AND STEWS
Copyright © 2016 Georgia Varozza
Published by Harvest House Publishers
Eugene, Oregon 97402
www.harvesthousepublishers.com

ISBN 978-0-7369-6329-9 (pbk.)
ISBN 978-0-7369-6330-5 (eBook)

Library of Congress Cataloging-in-Publication Data
    Names: Varozza, Georgia, 1953- author.
    Title: 99 favorite Amish soups and stews / Georgia Varozza.
    Other titles: Ninety-nine favorite Amish soups and stews
    Description: Eugene, Oregon : Harvest House Publishers, [2016] | Includes
        index.
    Identifiers: LCCN 2015044103 | ISBN 9780736963299 (pbk.)
    Subjects: LCSH: Amish cooking. | Soup. | Stews. | LCGFT: Cookbooks.
    Classification: LCC TX721 .V2773 2016 | DDC 641.5/66—dc23 LC record available
    at http://lccn.loc.gov/2015044103

Printed in China

    16 17 18 19 20 21 22 23 24 / RDS-KBD / 10 9 8 7 6 5 4 3 2 1

To my family—
My richest treasure on earth.
Walker, Travis, Logan, Sara, Crystalynn
Audrey, Asher, Easton, Alexis, Everett

To God—
My richest treasure in life.
You and I know that
I can do nothing without You.

But the glorious truth is that "I can do everything
through Christ, who gives me strength"
(Philippians 4:13 NLT).

CONTENTS

AMISH SOUPS AND STEWS—
A GREAT ADDITION TO YOUR
MEAL PLANNING
7

SOUPS
9

STEWS
63

A LITTLE SOMETHING EXTRA
117

RECIPE INDEX
121

SOUPS

STEWS

A LITTLE
SOMETHING EXTRA

AMISH SOUPS AND STEWS—A GREAT ADDITION TO YOUR MEAL PLANNING

To me, homemade soups and stews speak of home and comfort. I think many of us think of making soups and stews during the cooler months of late autumn through early spring, but really, soups and stews make a fine meal any day of the year. Serve with a salad and bread of some kind, and you have a nutritious and filling meal. And because many of these recipes seem to cook themselves, it's easy to go about your routine and still have a hot meal waiting to nourish your loved ones at the end of a busy day.

Amish cooks are known for their straightforward, tasty recipes—no fancy ingredients, and often the list of ingredients is minimal. These women are adept at using what they have on hand or in season, so soups and stews are a perfect choice for using up bits and pieces. Of course, when they butcher a chicken, cow, or hog, the choices widen considerably, but a fine soup can be made without any meat. Another reason I love Amish recipes for soups and stews is because leftovers are perfect to pack in a thermos or microwavable container and eat for lunch the next day. They reheat beautifully. Add a piece or two of buttered bread, and you'll be set.

I think you'll find some new favorites among the choices in this book. And let's face it—there's nothing much better than having your loved ones walk into the house after a long day and immediately smell tantalizing aromas coming from the kitchen.

My prayer for you is that—like the Amish strive to do—you'll find great joy in the simple pleasures of home, seeking to "lead a quiet and peaceable life in all godliness and honesty" (1 Timothy 2:2 KJV).

Georgia

SOUPS

When you think of homemade soup, you probably envision chicken noodle or old-fashioned vegetable. Both of these are tried-and-true recipes, but the choices you'll find in this section offer so much more than just those two standbys.

If you are planning to feed children, make a large batch of Potato Rivel Soup. I've yet to meet a child who doesn't like it, and big eaters will be satisfied as well because it's stick-to-the-ribs filling. Give the Chicken Corn Chowder a try if you're in the mood for a tasty twist from the ordinary. Mock Oyster Soup—made with salsify instead of oysters—is quintessentially Amish, as is the Amish Bean Soup. With 50 soup recipes to consider, I'm confident you can find some new family favorites. I hope you'll give them a try.

Jesus answered, "It is written:
'Man shall not live on bread alone,
but on every word that comes from the mouth of God.'"

MATTHEW 4:4

- - - - - - - - - -

Dear Lord, as I work in the kitchen preparing
meals for my loved ones, help me to remember
always that Your Word is what truly feeds my family.
Help me to point the way to You in everything
I do and with everyone I meet. Your "bread" is
life to the soul for all who come to You through
Christ, and I don't want anyone to hunger and
miss out on eternal life in Your glorious, perfect
presence. Use me, Father, as You will, and may I
be found a willing and cheerful follower. Amen.

1 Amish Bean Soup

½ cube (4 T.) butter
½ cup diced onions
½ cup celery, diced
1 quart cooked navy or great northern beans
2 T. seasoned salt (just use salt and pepper and maybe a bit of
    garlic powder if you don't have seasoned salt)
2-3 quarts milk
bread cubes (about ½ cup per bowl)

In a large pot, melt the butter; add the onions and celery and cook, stirring, until the onions are translucent. Add the beans and seasoned salt, stir gently, and cook on medium-low until heated through, stirring regularly so the beans don't stick to the bottom of the pot. Add the milk and heat, stirring regularly, until the soup is hot.

Add bread cubes to individual serving bowls and ladle soup over the top. You can use any kind of bread you wish, but our family likes plain, homemade white bread the best with this recipe.

Notes:

2 Barley Soup

1 lb. beef stew meat, cubed
1½ quarts water or beef broth
¾ cup barley, rinsed
2 onions, chopped
3 carrots, peeled and sliced
2 turnips, peeled and chopped
1 14½-ounce can diced tomatoes (or use a pint jar of home-
   canned tomatoes)
salt and pepper to taste

In a large pot or Dutch oven, brown beef cubes in a small amount of oil. Add the water (or broth) and barley and bring to a boil; reduce heat and simmer, covered, for 1 hour or until the barley is tender. Add the onions, carrots, turnips, and diced tomatoes. Cover the pot and simmer until the carrots are tender, or as long as another hour. Season with salt and pepper to taste. You can add more water or broth if too much has evaporated during cooking or if you want to stretch the number of servings.

Notes:

3 Beef and Barley Soup

½ lb. hamburger
1 cup carrots, peeled and finely diced
1 stalk celery, finely diced
¼ cup onion, peeled and finely diced
½ cup pearled or scotch barley (also called pot barley)
2 quarts beef broth
salt and pepper to taste

Brown hamburger and drain off fat. Combine all ingredients and simmer, covered, until barley is tender, about one hour, depending on the type of barley used.

Note: Pearled barley has been polished to remove the bran. Scotch (or pot) barley has also been polished, but to a lesser degree, so some of the bran is still intact. Due to the lighter processing, scotch or pot barley takes a bit longer than pearled barley to completely cook.

Notes:

4 Beef and Green Bean Soup

This is a great recipe if you have a small amount of leftover roast beef or some stew meat.

4 cups beef broth
1 cup cooked beef, cubed
2 potatoes, peeled and diced
2 carrots, peeled and sliced
1 stalk celery, sliced
1 small onion, diced
¼-½ tsp. thyme
¼-½ tsp. rosemary
1 can green beans (I use a pint or pint-and-a-half jar of home
    canned.)
1 cup whipping cream or evaporated milk
salt and pepper to taste

In a pot, add the beef broth and bring to a boil; add the beef, potatoes, carrots, celery, onion, thyme, and rosemary. Simmer, covered, for about 30 minutes or until the vegetables are tender. Add the green beans and taste the broth to see if you need to add salt and/or pepper. Continue to simmer for about 5-10 minutes or longer. Just before serving, lower the heat and add the cream; heat thoroughly but do not boil.

Notes:

5 Beefy Onion Rivel Soup

For soup:
¼ cup (½ stick) butter
2 cups thinly sliced onions
6 cups beef broth

For rivels:
1 egg
½ tsp. salt
pepper to taste
1 cup flour

In a large pot, melt the butter and add the onions. Cook the onions on fairly low heat until they are lightly browned and tender. Add the broth; raise the heat to medium-high and bring the broth and onions to a boil.

While the broth is coming to a boil, prepare the rivels as follows: In a medium mixing bowl, beat the egg well. Add the salt, and pepper if using, and stir well again. Add the flour and mix. I usually begin the process with a fork and then finish mixing with my hands. The dough won't be completely stuck together and smooth—this is what you want. The rivels should be small, no bigger than the size of a large pea. Sprinkle the rivels into the boiling broth, stirring constantly while adding them so they don't stick together. When all the rivels are in, reduce the heat, cover the pot, and simmer for about 10 minutes. Don't peek!

Notes:

6 Boiled Potpie Soup

2 eggs
⅔ cup milk
½ tsp. salt
3 cups flour
3 quarts beef, chicken, or vegetable broth
1 small onion, peeled and thinly sliced
4 potatoes, peeled and thinly sliced
1 tsp. parsley
salt and pepper to taste (may not need any)

To make potpie squares: In a large mixing bowl, beat the eggs; add the milk and salt. Stir to mix. Add the flour and mix until a ball of dough forms. (I usually mix with my hands to be sure everything is fully combined, but you don't want to overmix.) Roll out the dough into thin sheets and then cut into 3-inch squares. (A pizza cutter works great for this!)

To make the potpie soup: Bring the broth, onion, and parsley to a boil in a large soup pot. (This recipe works better in a pot that is wider rather than taller.) After the broth is boiling, begin adding the dough squares and potatoes in layers until all are added. Cover the pot, lower the heat a bit, and cook for 5 minutes. Stir gently and then continue to cook on low to medium-low until squares are cooked—about 15 minutes more.

Note: The trick to making this soup come out well is to make sure the dough squares, onions, and potatoes are *thinly* sliced so they cook quickly.

Notes:

7 Cabbage and Apple Soup

2½ cups chicken broth
2½ cups water
1 can tomato sauce (8 ounces, or 1 cup)
2 tsp. lemon juice
3 cups cabbage
2 cups apples, peeled and diced
¼ cup onions, diced
1 T. caraway seeds
1 clove garlic, crushed, or ¼ tsp. garlic powder
pinch of sugar
salt and pepper to taste

In a large pot, combine the chicken broth, water, tomato sauce, and lemon juice. Stir well to mix. Bring to a boil and then add the remainder of the ingredients. Gently simmer, stirring occasionally, until apples and cabbage are tender, about 30 minutes. Adjust seasonings and serve.

This soup tastes good as is, with the apples as a surprising addition. For an even heartier meal, you can also brown a bit of hamburger, drain off the grease, and add it to the soup.

Notes:

8 Cabbage and Vegetable Chowder

3 cups water
4 cups cabbage, coarsely shredded
2 cups carrots, peeled and thinly sliced
3 cups potatoes, peeled and diced
1 T. salt
½ tsp. sugar
¼ tsp. pepper
4 cups scalded milk (see note)
2 T. butter

In a large soup pot, add the water, cabbage, carrots, potatoes, salt, sugar, and pepper. Make sure there is enough water to cover the vegetables while they are cooking; you can add a bit more water to keep them covered. Cook until all vegetables are tender. Add the scalded milk and butter and heat thoroughly, but do not boil.

Note: To scald milk, use a separate saucepan and bring the milk to just under boiling on medium heat, stirring frequently so it doesn't scorch on the bottom. Remove from heat and allow to cool (although for this soup you don't need to worry about this last step; the milk can still be hot when you add it to the vegetables).

Notes:

9 Cabbage, Bean, and Ham Soup

2½ cups coarsely chopped or shredded cabbage
2 15-ounce cans navy beans, drained, rinsed, and drained again
1 cup chopped, cooked ham
1 cup onions, diced
2 carrots, peeled and thickly sliced
1 cup chopped turnips (about 1 medium-sized turnip, peeled)
1 tsp. marjoram
¼ tsp. pepper
1 bay leaf
6 cups water

In a large soup pot, add all ingredients and stir to mix. Bring to a boil and then lower the heat, cover the pot, and cook until vegetables are tender. Discard the bay leaf, taste and adjust seasonings as necessary (it will probably need salt, depending on how much and what kind of ham you used), and serve.

Notes:

10 **Carrot and Sweet Potato Cream Soup**

2 tsp. oil or butter
⅓ cup onions or shallots, chopped
1½ cups carrots, peeled and sliced
3 cups sweet potatoes, peeled and cubed
½ tsp. ginger powder
2 tsp. curry powder
¼ tsp. garlic powder
3 cups chicken broth
salt and pepper to taste

In a soup pot, melt the butter or pour in oil and add the onion; sauté for several minutes or until the onion is beginning to soften and look translucent. Add the carrots, sweet potatoes, ginger, curry, and garlic powder, and sauté, stirring, for several minutes longer. Add the broth and bring to a boil. Reduce heat, cover, and simmer until the vegetables are tender, about a half hour.

When the veggies are tender, your next step is to cream the soup. You can do this several ways:

- Use a food processor and blend about half at a time.

- Use an eggbeater and go at it until well blended and creamy. You'll need a heavy-duty eggbeater for this, and I wouldn't suggest any plastic parts because it'll be hot. (I use and highly recommend an Amish-made eggbeater available from www. cottagecraftworks.com. Although it's expensive, it's a workhorse.)

- Use a blender, remembering to keep the top covered to avoid splashing. (I happen to use a hand-cranked Vortex blender. No electricity needed, and it works nicely.)

Notes:

When you are finished creaming the soup, return it to the pot and reheat it. Taste the soup and add salt and pepper as desired. When you serve the soup, a nice dollop of sour cream or unflavored yogurt spooned on top is an extra taste treat, but it's not necessary.

11 Celery Soup

3 cups celery, diced
½ cup onion, diced
2 cups chicken broth
1 cup water
2 T. butter
2 T. flour
2 cups milk
1 cup cream or half-and-half
salt and pepper to taste

In a soup pot, mix together the celery, onion, chicken broth, and water. Simmer until the celery and onion are tender. At this point you can put the soup through a sieve if you want a creamy soup, but it's not necessary, especially if you have finely diced the vegetables.

In a medium saucepan, melt the butter and add the flour, stirring constantly. Add the milk and continue to stir constantly until the mixture has thickened slightly. Add to the soup and stir to mix well. Add the cream and salt and pepper to taste, and heat soup until hot but not boiling.

Some folks believe that celery is an excellent nerve tonic, so this might be the perfect soup to have on an especially hectic day.

Notes:

12 Cheddar Cheese Soup with Pumpernickel Croutons

4 slices pumpernickel bread, cut into cubes
¼ cup butter
1 medium onion, finely diced
¼ cup flour
3 cups chicken broth
3 cups milk
4 cups shredded Cheddar cheese
salt and pepper to taste

Place the bread cubes on a cookie sheet in an oven set at 200º and let them dry out and get a bit crisp while you're making the soup. (You can also butter the bread before baking the cubes. It's tasty but not necessary.) Check them occasionally and stir them so all sides are exposed.

In a soup pot, melt the butter, add the onion, and cook until the onion is soft and translucent. Add the flour and cook, stirring constantly, until all ingredients have been thoroughly mixed together. Gradually add the chicken broth and cook, still stirring constantly, until the mixture has thickened slightly. Add the milk and continue to cook until the soup is very hot—just under the boiling point. Turn off the heat and add the Cheddar cheese; stir until cheese is completely melted. (You may need to turn the stove back on low heat for a bit if you have trouble getting all the cheese to melt.) Add salt and pepper to taste.

Remove the pumpernickel croutons from the oven if you haven't already done so and place them in a serving bowl that you can bring to the table. Ladle soup into individual bowls and sprinkle some of the croutons on top.

Notes:

13 Cheeseburger Soup

½ lb. ground beef
4 T. butter, divided
¾ cup onion, diced
¾ cup carrots, peeled and thinly sliced or diced
¾ cup celery, diced
3 cups chicken broth
4 cups potatoes, peeled and cubed
1 tsp. parsley flakes
¼ cup flour
1 cup Cheddar cheese, shredded
1½ cups milk
¾ tsp. salt
¼ tsp. pepper
¼ cup sour cream

In a large pot brown beef; drain and set meat aside. In the same pot, add 1 tablespoon of the butter and gently sauté the onion, carrots, and celery, stirring occasionally so the vegetables don't burn and until they are tender, about 10 minutes. Add broth, potatoes, browned hamburger meat, and parsley. Bring mixture to a boil and then reduce heat, cover, and simmer for about 15 minutes or until the potatoes are tender.

Meanwhile, in a small sauté pan, melt remaining 3 tablespoons butter on low heat. Add flour and cook for 1-2 minutes, whisking constantly, until the mixture is bubbly. Pour the flour mixture into the soup pot and reduce the heat for the pot to low. Add the cheese and stir until it's melted. Add the milk and salt and pepper and heat until hot but not boiling. Remove from heat and stir in sour cream. When you serve the soup, you can also add a dollop of sour cream in each bowl if desired.

Notes:

14 Cheesy Onion Soup

3 T. butter
1 large onion, peeled and chopped
3 T. flour
½ tsp. salt
pepper to taste
4 cups milk
2 cups Cheddar (shredded) or Velveeta (cubed) cheese

In a saucepan or pot, melt the butter and then add the onion. Sauté for several minutes until onion is somewhat translucent; stir in the flour, salt, and some pepper, stirring or whisking constantly. Gradually add the milk, still stirring constantly. Bring to a low boil and cook for about 2 minutes or until slightly thickened. Continue gently stirring, making sure to touch all of the pan bottom with your stirring spoon so that the milk doesn't scorch. (The secret to creamy, lump-free white sauce or creamy soups is constant stirring.) Add the cheese and stir until melted.

Sometimes I add a bit of ground mustard, and we occasionally eat it with dried, seasoned bread cubes strewn on top. (You can buy croutons if you don't want to make your own.)

Notes:

15 Chicken Broth with Soda Cracker Dumplings

1 egg
2 T. butter, melted and slightly cooled
6 T. finely crushed soda cracker (commonly called saltines)
    crumbs
1 T. milk
¼ tsp. parsley
1 tsp. finely minced onion
¼ tsp. celery salt
dash of pepper
2 quarts chicken broth

To make the dumplings: In a medium-sized mixing bowl, add the egg and beat it well. Stir in the melted butter. Add the remaining ingredients—except the broth—and mix well. Using your hands and squeezing so the mixture sticks together well, shape into dumplings that are about the size of a small, unshelled walnut. Lay them out on a plate or towel for 30 minutes to give them time to meld. (As the cracker crumb dumplings sit, the crumbs will become saturated by the liquids and swell slightly.)

Pour the broth into a large pot and bring to a simmer. Drop the cracker dumplings into the broth and immediately reduce the heat to medium-low. Cover the pot and cook for 10 minutes without lifting the lid. Serve immediately.

Notes:

16 Chicken Chowder with Mushrooms

¾ lb. boneless, skinless chicken, cut into bite-sized pieces
2½ cups chicken broth
3 carrots, peeled and diced
2 stalks celery, chopped
1 small onion, diced
½ cup fresh mushrooms, sliced (I use button mushrooms)
½ tsp. parsley
¼ tsp. rosemary
1 T. butter
3 T. flour
1 cup milk
1 cup peas (fresh or frozen)

In a large soup pot, add the chicken and broth, bring to a boil, and simmer until the chicken is cooked through. Because the pieces of chicken are small, this won't take more than about 5 minutes. Using a slotted spoon, remove the cooked chicken and set aside for now.

Add the carrots, celery, onion, mushrooms, parsley, and rosemary to the pot and bring to a boil once again. Lower the heat, cover the pot, and simmer until the vegetables are tender, about 10-15 minutes.

Again using the slotted spoon, transfer about half of the cooked vegetables to a food processor or blender and puree. Return the pureed vegetables to the soup pot along with the cooked chicken, and keep the heat on fairly low—you don't want the soup to boil but you do want it to be hot.

In a small saucepan, melt the butter and add the flour, stirring constantly. Cook and stir for about 30 seconds and then—still stirring

Notes:

constantly—gradually add the milk. Cook until the mixture thickens and then add it to the soup, along with the peas. Simmer for several minutes more until the peas are hot. If you use frozen peas, you'll have to simmer the soup for a bit longer.

Before serving, add salt and pepper to taste.

17 Chicken, Corn, and Noodle Soup

1 roasting chicken (about 2½-3 lbs.)
2 T. butter
6 cups water
4 cups chicken broth
1 onion, peeled and quartered
3 celery ribs, cut in thirds
2 tsp. salt
1 tsp. pepper, scant
½ tsp. turmeric
1-2 cups frozen corn
4 cups cooked egg noodles (about 8 ounces uncooked)
3 hard-boiled eggs, coarsely chopped
parsley for garnish

In a large stockpot, melt the butter and brown the chicken; you can leave the chicken whole, or cut into pieces if desired. Add 6 cups water along with chicken broth, onion, celery, salt, pepper, and turmeric. Bring to a boil and then cover and reduce heat. Cook until chicken is tender. Remove the chicken, straining and reserving the broth, and let the chicken cool enough so that you can handle it; take the meat off the bones and place back into the stockpot with the broth. Bring the soup back to a gentle boil. Add the corn; simmer for about 5-10 minutes or until the corn is cooked through. Add the noodles and

Notes:

simmer for about another 5 minutes or so or until the noodles are hot. Taste the soup and add more salt or pepper if needed.

Serve garnished with hard-boiled eggs and parsley (fresh or dehydrated).

18 Chicken Corn Chowder

¼ cup butter
½ onion, diced
1 clove garlic, minced
2 potatoes, peeled and cubed in small pieces
1 carrot, peeled and diced
2½ cups chicken broth
4 ounces cream cheese, softened to nearly room temperature
1 14½-ounce can diced tomatoes, undrained
2 cups cooked chicken, cubed (I like a fairly small dice to match
     the size of the veggies)
1 tsp. dill weed (*not* dill seed)
1½ cups half-and-half or a combination of half-and-half and
     heavy cream
1 cup Cheddar cheese, shredded
2 cups corn, fresh or frozen

In a large pot, melt the butter and sauté the onion and garlic until the onion is translucent. Add the potatoes, carrot, and chicken broth and simmer for about 15 minutes or until the potatoes and carrot pieces are cooked through. Add a bit more broth or water if it boils down very much.

While the vegetables are simmering, in a medium-sized mixing bowl, mix together the cream cheese and diced tomatoes; use a fork to smash

Notes:

the cream cheese into the tomatoes. It won't be entirely smooth, but do your best. When the vegetables are cooked through, add the cream cheese mixture to the soup and stir. Next, add the chicken, dill, half-and-half, Cheddar cheese, and corn and stir until the cheese is melted. Heat the soup on low for about 20 minutes, stirring occasionally and not allowing it to boil.

19 Chili Bean Soup

½ lb. hamburger
1 small onion, diced
1 14½-ounce can diced tomatoes, undrained
2 cups water
1 can kidney or pinto beans (or use a pint jar of home-canned beans)
1 cup corn, fresh or frozen
1 cup tomato sauce
1 tsp. chili powder
salt and pepper to taste

In a pot, sauté the hamburger and onion until the hamburger has browned completely; drain off fat. Add remainder of ingredients and simmer for about 30 minutes. You can add a bit more water if you want your soup thinner.

Ladle into individual bowls and serve as is, or add shredded Cheddar cheese, sour cream, or broken tortilla chips on top.

Notes:

20 Cold Fruit Soup

2 quarts cold milk
¾ cup brown sugar
1 tsp. vanilla
4 cups fresh fruit, cut into bite-sized pieces
Bread, cut into bite-sized pieces (use the amount that seems
right, about 4 cups)

Mix together the milk, sugar, and vanilla. Let it set for a bit and then stir again so the brown sugar can dissolve at least a little. Place bread cubes and some fruit pieces in individual soup bowls and ladle the milk mixture over top.

Note: This makes a great meal on hot days, or when you are canning fruit. Just use the fruit-of-the-day, and you have a quick and easy lunch or dinner in minutes.

Notes:

21 Corn and Clam Chowder

2 slices bacon, cut into small pieces
3 potatoes, peeled and cut into bite-sized pieces
¾ cup onion, diced
½ cup celery, diced
2 cups milk
2 cans (6½ ounces each) minced clams, drained with liquid
     reserved
¾ tsp. thyme
⅛ tsp. pepper
1 15-ounce can or 1 pint jar homemade creamed corn
1 11-ounce can or 1 pint jar home-canned corn, drained

In a large pot, cook the bacon until brown and crisp. Use a slotted spoon to transfer the cooked bacon onto paper towels.

Add the potatoes, onion, and celery to the bacon drippings in the pot and cook, gently stirring (so veggies don't stick to the bottom), for 5 minutes. Add the milk, reserved clam juice, thyme, and pepper. Mix well, reduce heat to medium-low, cover the pot, and simmer for about 20 minutes or until potatoes are tender.

Take 2 cups of the vegetable mixture and puree until smooth, using either a food processor or blender. Return the pureed vegetables to the soup pot and then add the creamed corn, regular corn, and clams. Return the soup to a boil and then reduce the heat and simmer until completely hot, about 5 minutes.

To serve, ladle soup into individual bowls and sprinkle some of the cooked bacon on top of each bowl. (Alternatively, you can simply add the bacon to the soup pot and stir to mix before ladling the soup into individual bowls.)

Notes:

22 Corn and Tomato Chowder

4 slices bacon, chopped
2 T. celery, minced
2 T. bell pepper, minced
3 T. onion, minced
2 potatoes, peeled and diced
3 tomatoes, skinned and chopped
2 cups corn (use fresh or frozen)
1 cup water
4 cups milk
salt and pepper to taste
fresh parsley for garnish, chopped (optional)

Slightly brown the bacon in a soup pot. Add the celery, bell pepper, and onion and continue to brown the bacon until done, stirring so the vegetables don't stick to the bottom of the pot. The bacon grease can remain in the soup, but if you want to cut the amount, soak up some of the grease with paper towels before adding the potatoes, tomatoes, and corn along with 1 cup water. Cover pot and simmer on medium-low to low heat for 30 minutes. Add the milk and heat until almost boiling, but do not boil. Add salt and pepper to taste. Sprinkle a bit of fresh parsley on the top of each bowl if desired.

Notes:

23 Cottage Cheese and Vegetable Soup

1 cup celery, diced
1 cup onion, diced
3 cups broccoli, chopped
1 cup cottage cheese
1 can cream of chicken soup
2 cups milk
½ tsp. salt
⅛ tsp. pepper

In a large pot, cook celery, onion, and broccoli in just enough water to cover vegetables. Simmer until the vegetables are tender and do not drain the water.

Blend together the cottage cheese and cream of chicken soup until well mixed and smooth. Add the milk, salt, and pepper and mix well again. Add this mixture to the undrained vegetables and heat thoroughly, but do not boil. Adjust seasonings and serve.

Note: I sometimes add carrots and less broccoli. Really, you can add whatever vegetables in whatever amounts you'd like, as long as the total amount of veggies is around 5 cups in all.

Notes:

24 Creamy Broccoli and Carrot Soup

3 T. butter
2 T. onion, minced
3 T. flour
1¼ tsp. salt
3 cups milk
3 cups chicken broth
2 cups fresh broccoli, chopped
2 cups carrots, peeled and thinly sliced
salt and pepper to taste

Melt butter in a pot. Add onion and sauté until onions are tender. Stir in flour and salt and gradually add milk while stirring constantly. When the mixture has begun to boil and thicken slightly, add the broth, broccoli, and carrots. Heat over low heat for about 25 minutes, being careful not to let the soup boil; stir occasionally so vegetables don't stick to the bottom of the pot. Add salt and pepper to taste, and serve.

Notes:

25 Creamy Cabbage and Bacon Soup

½ lb. bacon, coarsely chopped
1 onion, chopped
12 cups cabbage, coarsely shredded
2½ quarts chicken broth
1 cup half-and-half
2 tsp. salt
½ tsp. pepper
Swiss, Cheddar, or Jack cheese, shredded, for garnish

In a large soup pot, fry the bacon pieces until crisp; remove the bacon with a slotted spoon and set aside but don't drain the grease. Add the onion to the bacon grease and sauté for 5-10 minutes, stirring occasionally, until the onion is translucent; add the cabbage and, stirring occasionally, continue to sauté for another 5 minutes or so until the cabbage is limp but not browned. Add the broth and simmer until the cabbage and onions are tender, about 15 minutes. Add the half-and-half, salt, and pepper, and heat thoroughly but do not boil.

Sprinkle the bacon pieces and cheese on top of each bowl of soup. (We do this at the table so everyone can add the amount that seems right to them.)

Notes:

26 Creamy Carrot and Rice Soup

4-5 carrots, peeled and grated
1 onion, peeled and minced
4 cups chicken or vegetable broth
1 cup cooked rice
3 T. butter
1 tsp. salt
1 T. sugar
1 cup milk

In a pot, add the carrots and onion with enough water to cover. Cook until soft. (It won't take long.) Drain off water. Add the broth, cooked rice, butter, salt, and sugar and heat until hot. Add the milk and continue to heat on low until the soup is hot enough to serve.

Optional: You can puree some or all of this soup if you like it creamy and smooth. I also sometimes add a bit of powdered ginger or turmeric for extra flavor and color, but it's good as is.

Notes:

27 Creamy Corn Chowder

1 small onion, finely chopped
2 stalks celery, finely chopped
4 T. butter
4 cups chicken broth
4 potatoes, peeled and cut in bite-sized pieces
2 tsp. salt
1 tsp. pepper
1 clove garlic, minced
1 tsp. parsley flakes, or 1 T. fresh parsley, minced
2 quarts frozen (thawed) or fresh corn
1 cup half-and-half
3 cups milk

In a large soup pot, sauté onion and celery in butter until onion is translucent, about 5 minutes. Add the chicken broth, potatoes, salt, pepper, garlic, and parsley and simmer for 30 minutes. Add the corn and simmer gently for another 15 minutes or so. Add the half-and-half and milk and heat thoroughly but do not boil. Adjust seasonings and serve.

Note: Many times I've decided on corn chowder for dinner and simply used frozen corn if I didn't have time to thaw it beforehand. The soup is just as good, but taste several kernels to be certain the corn has been completely cooked before adding the half-and-half and milk.

Notes:

28 Egg Soup

6 cups chicken broth
¼ cup uncooked white rice
4 eggs
3 T. lemon juice
3 hard-boiled eggs, diced

In a soup pot, heat broth and rice to boiling. Reduce heat to low, cover pot, and cook for about 20 minutes or until rice is cooked.

In a medium mixing bowl add the eggs and lemon and, using a hand beater or a whisk, beat the mixture until frothy.

Reduce the heat for the soup to the lowest setting. Stir a small amount of the hot broth into the egg mixture and then, stirring constantly, pour the egg mixture into the pot of simmering soup. Continue to stir constantly until the soup is heated through but not boiling. Just before serving, taste and add salt or pepper if needed.

Ladle the soup into individual bowls and sprinkle hard-boiled eggs on top.

Note: You can purchase a heavy-duty eggbeater made by Amish craftsmen from www.cottagecraftworks.com. Although it's fairly expensive, it has proven to be an indispensable addition in my kitchen. Other, cheaper eggbeaters have plastic parts and aren't as big, so they don't last as long or work as well for larger batches of food that need whipping.

Notes:

29 Farmer's Favorite Soup

1 lb. hamburger
1 onion, chopped
1 cup celery, chopped
2 potatoes, peeled and diced (at least 1 cup, but more is better
     in my opinion)
1 cup carrots, peeled and sliced or diced
salt and pepper to taste
1 cup tomato sauce
2½ quarts water
¼ cup cornmeal
¼ cup water

In the large soup pot or Dutch oven you plan on making soup in, brown the hamburger and onion together; drain off grease. Add the celery, potatoes, carrots, salt and pepper, tomato sauce, and 2½ quarts water. Simmer, covered, until vegetables are tender.

When soup is done, mix together the cornmeal and ¼ cup water. Add to the soup, stirring so that lumps don't form. Continue stirring until soup is slightly thickened, about 2 minutes.

Note: When my youngest son was just a little squirt, we were at the dinner table eating this soup (it's a family favorite), and my little guy piped up with what he considered supreme praise. He said, "Mama, this soup is as good as Campbell's!" We all laughed, and I was well pleased to accept such a sincere compliment. If you have little ones who think Campbell's soup tastes good, this is sure to be a hit at your house as well.

Notes:

30 Hamburger Soup

1 lb. hamburger
1 cup onion, peeled and chopped
1 cup potatoes, peeled and chopped
1 cup carrots, peeled and sliced thin or chopped
1 cup cabbage, shredded
1 cup celery, chopped
4 cups tomatoes, peeled and chopped
¼ cup rice, uncooked
3-4 cups water or beef broth
4 tsp. salt (use less if you use broth instead of water)
¼ tsp. basil
¼ tsp. thyme
1 large bay leaf

Brown hamburger and onion together; drain off grease. Add remaining ingredients and simmer, covered, until vegetables are tender and rice is cooked, about 25 minutes. Remove bay leaf and serve.

Notes:

31 Leek and Potato Soup

3-4 good-sized leeks
2 T. butter
4 cups chicken or vegetable broth
2 lbs. potatoes, peeled and diced
1 tsp. salt
½ tsp. pepper, scant
¼ tsp. marjoram
½ tsp. thyme
1 bay leaf
½ cup heavy cream or half-and-half

Clean leeks well. Cut them lengthwise in half or quarters (depending on size) and then rinse well to get rid of any sand or soil still clinging to them. Using only the white and light green portions, thinly chop the leeks.

Melt butter over low heat in a heavy soup pot; add the chopped leeks, cover the pot, and cook on low for about 10 minutes or until the leeks are softened but not browned. Occasionally remove the lid and stir the leeks gently to check for browning.

Add broth, potatoes, salt, pepper, marjoram, thyme, and the bay leaf. Simmer the soup for 20 minutes, stirring occasionally, until the potatoes are soft. Using a potato masher or ricer, mash the soup to break up some of the potatoes and make a creamier soup. You can mash more or less depending on how chunky you like your soup. Add the cream and heat but don't boil. Taste and add more salt and pepper if desired.

Ladle soup into individual bowls and eat plain or garnish with croutons, a dollop of sour cream, or shredded Parmesan or Cheddar cheese.

Notes:

32 Lentil Soup

5 cups broth or water (beef broth tastes especially good in this
    recipe)
1 cup lentils
1 onion, diced
2 stalks celery, diced
2 large carrots, peeled and diced
1 clove garlic, minced
1 large potato, peeled and diced
2 cups tomato sauce (I use a pint jar of my homemade sauce)
½ tsp. curry powder
½ tsp. basil
salt and pepper to taste

Combine all ingredients in a large pot and simmer for 1-2 hours.
Adjust seasonings and serve.

Notes:

33 Meat and Potatoes Soup with Hard-Boiled Eggs

1-1½ lbs. hamburger
6 large potatoes, peeled and cubed into bite-sized pieces
1 onion, peeled and diced
1 stalk celery, diced or thinly sliced
salt and pepper to taste
1 14½-ounce can diced tomatoes, including liquid (or use a pint
    jar of home-canned tomatoes)
2 hard-boiled eggs, chopped
parsley for garnish (optional)

In a large soup pot, brown the hamburger; drain off fat. Add the potatoes, onion, and celery and enough water or broth to cover all ingredients. (The more liquid you use, the more people you can feed.) Add salt and pepper to taste. Simmer until the potatoes are cooked. Add the diced tomatoes and continue to simmer until ready to serve. (Let it simmer long enough for the diced tomatoes to become hot, or you can let it simmer for a bit longer if necessary.)

When ready to serve, ladle soup into individual bowls and add hard-boiled egg and parsley (if using) on top of the soup in each bowl.

Notes:

34 Meatball Soup

2 lbs. hamburger
2 tsp. salt
⅛ tsp. pepper
2 eggs, beaten
¼ cup chopped fresh parsley (or use 1 T. dried parsley flakes)
½ cup crushed cracker crumbs or bread crumbs
2 T. milk
5 T. flour
2 small or 1 large onion, diced
2 cups celery, diced
4 cups potatoes, peeled and diced
¼ cup uncooked white rice
6 cups tomato juice or V-8 juice
6 cups water
1 T. sugar
1 tsp. salt
1½ cups frozen corn, or a mixture of corn and peas (you can also use fresh)

Combine the first 7 ingredients. Mix thoroughly with your hands and then form into balls the size of walnuts. Dredge the meatballs in the flour and brown them on all sides, using enough oil so they don't stick when cooking in the large pot you plan to make the soup in. When the meatballs have browned, add the remaining ingredients, except the corn. Bring the mixture to a boil, reduce heat, cover with a tight-fitting lid, and continue to cook until the vegetables are tender and the rice is cooked through. (This shouldn't take too long because your veggies have been diced into small pieces.) Add the corn last and cook for about 10 minutes more.

Note: Even though this soup includes vegetables, most kids love the idea of eating meatball soup.

Notes:

35 Mock Oyster (Salsify) Soup

1½ cups salsify, peeled and sliced (see note below)
1½ cups water
1 T. butter
1 quart milk or half-and-half (or a combination)
salt and pepper
Parmesan cheese (optional)

Cook the salsify until tender in the water to which you have added a pinch of salt. Add the butter and milk or half-and-half and bring to nearly boiling. Season to taste and serve. Feel free to pass the Parmesan cheese at the table along with fresh, chopped parsley.

Note: Salsify is also called "oyster plant" because of its vaguely similar taste to oysters. Salsify roots look a lot like carrots, except they are white or brown, depending on which variety you get. Scrub the roots before removing the skins and then remove any dark spots and trim the top and bottom of the roots before slicing. Also, salsify cooks faster than carrots, and it will become mushy if overcooked, so watch your pot carefully.

Notes:

36 Old-Fashioned Chicken Noodle Soup

1 3-4 lb. chicken
1 stalk celery, chunked into thirds
1 small onion, quartered
2 carrots, peeled and chopped or sliced
4 cups cooked noodles (about 8 ounces uncooked), drained
salt and pepper to taste

In a large pot, add the chicken, celery, and onion; cover with water to about 3 inches over the chicken. Cover the pot, bring to a boil, and then lower the heat to keep a slow simmer going. Boil the chicken until done, about 1½ hours. Remove the chicken from the pot and let it cool enough to handle. Strain the broth and return it to the soup pot; allow the broth to cool enough so that the fat rises to the top and then skim off as much fat as you can.

Turn the heat to about medium and bring the broth to simmering again. Prepare the carrots and add them to the broth. Cook them until soft.

In the meantime, remove the chicken from the bones and skin. Chop or shred the chicken into bite-sized pieces and add the pieces to the soup while the carrots are cooking. At this point, taste the soup and add salt and pepper and any other spices that sound good to you, such as thyme, summer savory, marjoram, oregano, etc. (I usually stick to just salt and pepper—we're purists in our family.) When the carrots are done, add the cooked noodles and continue to simmer for several minutes to heat thoroughly.

Notes:

37 Old-Fashioned Vegetable Beef Soup

¼ cup vegetable oil
1 small onion, diced
3 stalks celery, sliced
2 carrots, peeled and sliced
½ small head cabbage, coarsely shredded
1 zucchini, chopped
1½ lbs. beef suitable for stew, cut into bite-sized pieces
6 medium potatoes (or 4 large), peeled and diced
2 cans (14½ ounces each) diced tomatoes, undrained
6 cups water
1 can (16 ounces) cut green beans (don't use French-style) or 1
    pint jar home-canned green beans, drained
1 can (8 ounces) baby lima beans, drained
4 tsp. salt
½ tsp. pepper
½ tsp. basil

In a heavy-bottomed soup pot, add the oil, onion, celery, carrots, cabbage, and zucchini and cook until vegetables are lightly browned. With a slotted spoon, remove vegetables to a large bowl and set aside for now.

In the same pot and using what's left of the oil, cook the beef cubes, stirring frequently, until all pieces are well browned on all sides. Add the reserved cooked vegetables and all other ingredients and heat to boiling. Reduce heat to low, cover pot, and simmer for about 30 minutes or until the meat and potatoes are tender.

Notes:

Note: Some members of my family are not fans of lima beans, so I sometimes make this soup without them. Instead, I add a cup of frozen peas during the last few minutes of cooking. Sprinkle on a bit of fresh parsley if you have some on hand. It's a beautiful—and versatile—soup.

38 Potato and Velveeta Cheese Soup

6 cups potatoes, peeled and chopped
1 cup celery, chopped
1 cup carrots, peeled and chopped or thinly sliced
½ cup onion, chopped
2 tsp. parsley (dried or fresh)
1 tsp. salt
pepper to taste
2 chicken bouillon cubes
2 cups water
3 cups milk
4 T. flour
1 lb. Velveeta cheese, cubed

In a large pot, add the potatoes, celery, carrots, onion, parsley, salt, pepper, bouillon cubes, and water. Bring to a low boil and then turn down the heat and simmer for 20 minutes. (You might need to add a bit more water during the cooking time if it looks a little dry, but don't add too much.)

Blend together the milk and flour. (I put the milk and flour in a quart canning jar and cover tightly with a lid and then shake until it's blended.) Gradually add the milk mixture to the potato mixture, stirring constantly. Cook until the soup thickens. Add the cubed Velveeta

Notes:

cheese and continue to cook, stirring, until the cheese is melted. Adjust seasonings and serve.

Note: This is an easy soup as long as you have the ingredients on hand, and it makes a wonderful meal on a cold winter day. Velveeta cheese is shelf-stable and lasts for quite a long time, so you can always keep a box or two in your pantry.

39 Potato Rivel Soup

No cookbook would be complete in my opinion without a recipe for this easy and delicious Potato Rivel Soup. My kids were raised on it, and often requested this soup. I've never known a child to dislike this soup (although there have been a few who dislike onions so I sometimes "cheat" and instead of using diced onions, add a bit of onion powder for taste). It is filling and inexpensive, which to my way of thinking, is about the perfect meal. Please give it a try. I think you'll be so glad you did.

For soup:
3 lbs. potatoes, peeled and cubed (just guesstimate the amount)
½ cup onion, diced
pinch of salt
2 T. butter
salt and pepper to taste
1 cup milk
1 cup water

For rivels:
1 cup flour
½ tsp. salt
1 egg

Notes:

To make the soup: Put potatoes and onions in a large soup pot with enough water to barely cover them and a pinch of salt. Cook until the potatoes are done. Do not drain the water. Take a potato masher and roughly mash the potatoes in the water. (There will still be small lumps.) Then add the butter and salt and pepper to taste. Next, add the liquid—you need the combination of the milk and water because the milk gives the soup a creamy richness. Bring the soup to a gentle bubbling simmer.

To make the rivels: In a medium mixing bowl, mix together the flour and salt. Make an indentation in the middle of the flour mixture and break the egg into it. Using a fork, mix egg and flour mixture together until you have lumps about the size of grapes. This is a fairly messy process, so feel free to use your hands to finish mixing and separating the lumps until they are the right size. Drop the rivels into the soup and cook them until done, stirring occasionally, for about 10 minutes or so depending on their size. If the soup is too thick, you can add additional milk. Adjust the seasoning to taste before serving.

Notes:

40 Potato Soup with Celery and Eggs

2 cups potatoes, peeled and diced
1 onion, chopped
¼ cup celery, sliced
1 quart milk
salt and pepper to taste
3 hard-boiled eggs, shelled and chopped
2 T. butter
1 T. chopped fresh parsley

In a heavy pot, add 3 cups water, potatoes, onion, and celery; bring to a boil, reduce heat, and simmer until potatoes are cooked through.

Add the milk and heat on low until hot, but do not boil. Add salt and pepper to taste and then add the hard-boiled eggs, butter, and parsley. Serve as soon as the butter has melted, stirring to mix the butter and parsley before ladling into individual bowls.

Notes:

41 Pumpkin Soup

1 T. vegetable oil
½ lb. good quality beef stew meat, cubed into bite-sized pieces
1 small pie pumpkin, peeled and cut into ½-inch cubes
1 onion, chopped
3 cups beef broth
1 14½-ounce can diced tomatoes, undrained
¼ tsp. marjoram
¼ tsp. thyme
¼ tsp. hot pepper sauce (less if you don't like a lot of heat)
soy sauce (optional)

In a large pot, brown the beef cubes in the vegetable oil over medium-high heat. Transfer the meat to a plate and set aside. Reduce the heat to medium-low and then add the pumpkin and onion to the pot and cook for 15 minutes.

Return beef to the pot and add the broth, tomatoes, marjoram, thyme, and hot pepper sauce. Increase the heat to medium-high and bring the soup just to boiling. Cover the pot, lower the heat, and simmer the soup until pumpkin is tender, about another 20 minutes.

Ladle soup into individual bowls and serve. Bring the bottle of soy sauce to the table and let people put a few squirts into their soup if desired.

Notes:

SOUPS

42 Quick and Easy Tomato Soup

2 cans (6 ounces each) tomato paste
2 quarts water
2 stalks celery, chunked into thirds
1 tsp. salt (go easy on the salt; you can always add more later)
pepper to taste
¼ tsp. onion powder
⅛ tsp. garlic powder
¼ tsp. each oregano, basil, thyme, rosemary, and celery seed
1 T. sugar
1 bay leaf (optional, but good)
¼-⅓ cup milk, half-and-half, or heavy cream

In a large pot, mix together all ingredients except the milk; stir to mix well. Bring to a boil and then simmer for 20 minutes. Remove the celery pieces and bay leaf. Taste and adjust seasonings if needed.

Pour in the milk and heat the soup until hot but not boiling. Serve.

Note 1: You can eat the tomato soup without adding the milk if you desire.

Note 2: Here's what you can do if you want thicker soup: Before adding the milk to the soup, take a small saucepan and melt 1 tablespoon butter. Then add 1 tablespoon flour while stirring constantly. Into this gradually add about 1 cup of the tomato soup. Keep stirring while you wait for the mixture to thicken, and when it does, add the mixture into the soup pot and continue stirring. Then add the milk. Stir to mix and heat until hot but not boiling.

Notes:

43 Spaghetti Soup

1 lb. hamburger
½ cup onion, chopped
½ cup bell pepper, chopped
1 stalk celery, chopped
1 carrot, peeled and chopped
2 cloves garlic, minced
2 14½-ounce cans diced tomatoes (do not drain)
1 15-ounce can tomato sauce plus half of the can of water (this
   helps to get every last bit of tomato sauce)
2½ cups water
1 T. sugar
1 tsp. Italian seasoning
½ tsp. salt
¼ tsp. pepper
2 ounces uncooked spaghetti noodles, broken into small pieces
   (see note below)
Parmesan cheese for topping

In a large pot, add the hamburger, onion, bell pepper, celery, carrot, and garlic; brown the mixture until the hamburger is no longer pink. Drain off fat.

Add the undrained diced tomatoes, tomato sauce, water, sugar, Italian seasoning, salt, and pepper and bring to a boil. Add the noodles, return the soup to a boil, reduce heat, and simmer until the noodles are done, about 12 minutes. Adjust seasonings and serve. At the table let everyone add as much or as little Parmesan cheese as they desire.

Note: You don't need to weigh out the spaghetti noodles. Just grab a handful that is about 2¼ inches in circumference (the circumference is the distance around the outside edge of the circle).

Notes:

44 Split Pea Soup

1 cup dried split peas
12 cups water, divided
1 ham hock or pieces of cubed ham
1 carrot, peeled and finely diced
1 onion, peeled and finely diced
1 potato, peeled and finely diced
¼ cup celery, finely diced
¼ cup green bell pepper, finely diced (optional)
salt and pepper to taste

In a large pot, add peas and 6 cups boiling water; cover the pot and let soak for 1 hour. Then drain the water and add 6 cups of fresh water and remainder of ingredients. Bring to a boil and then lower the heat and simmer until peas are thoroughly cooked and tender (about 45 minutes, depending on how old the peas are). Add water during cooking time because split peas absorb water while cooking.

Note: You can make split pea soup (using this recipe) without soaking the peas first, but the soup will take longer to cook until the peas are tender—about 2 hours.

Notes:

45 Sweet Potato and Tortilla Chip Soup

1 T. vegetable oil
1 cup onion, chopped
2 cloves garlic, minced
4 sweet potatoes, peeled and cut into ½-inch cubes (4 cups total)
3 cups chicken broth
½ tsp. cumin
½ tsp. oregano
½ tsp. chili powder
¼ tsp. red pepper flakes or ground red pepper (use less if you don't like a lot of heat)
1 14½-ounce can diced tomatoes, including juice, or 1 pint jar home-canned tomatoes
1 cup fresh or frozen corn
1 4½-ounce can chopped green chilies
3 T. chopped fresh cilantro or parsley
tortilla chips, broken but not crushed

In a large pot, heat the oil and then add the onions and garlic. Cook, stirring occasionally, until onion is tender and translucent.

Stir in sweet potatoes, broth, cumin, oregano, chili powder, and red pepper. Bring to a boil and then reduce heat to low and simmer, covered, for about 20 minutes or until sweet potatoes are tender.

Using about 2 cups (more if you prefer a creamier soup), puree the soup in a food processor or blender until smooth and then return the mixture to the pot. Add the diced tomatoes, corn, green chilies, and cilantro to the soup and continue to cook over medium heat until the soup is heated thoroughly.

To serve, ladle soup into individual bowls and sprinkle with tortilla chips.

Notes:

46 Taco Soup

1 lb. hamburger
1 onion, chopped
1 bell pepper, chopped
1 cup corn, fresh or frozen
1 14½-ounce can diced tomatoes with green chilies (use 2 cans if
    you like it spicy), undrained
2 14½-ounce cans diced tomatoes, undrained
4 cans water
2 T. powdered Ranch Dressing mix
½ tsp. garlic powder
1½ tsp. cumin
¼ cup uncooked white rice
salt and pepper to taste

In a large soup pot, brown the hamburger; drain fat. Add remaining ingredients and simmer until the rice is cooked through, about 25 minutes.

We like this soup with shredded Cheddar cheese sprinkled on top. Or try adding broken tortilla chips or a dollop of sour cream.

Notes:

47 Turnip Soup

4 cups milk
1 onion, peeled and cut in half
2 T. butter
1 T. flour
2 cups grated turnips
1 tsp. salt
2 T. chopped fresh parsley

In the top of a double boiler add the milk and onion; heat until it begins to simmer, but don't let it come to a full boil.

Rub together the butter and flour to make a paste. Add the paste to the milk mixture while stirring. Add the grated turnips and salt, and cook while you continue stirring until the turnips are soft, about 10-12 minutes.

Just before serving, remove the onion and stir in the parsley.

Notes:

48 Vegetable Soup

3 T. butter
1 small onion, chopped
1 stalk celery, thinly sliced
2 carrots, peeled and sliced or chopped
1 large potato, peeled and cut into bite-sized pieces
2 large tomatoes, peeled, seeded, and chopped
4 cups chicken or vegetable broth
1 tsp. basil
½ small head cauliflower or broccoli, broken into flowerets (or a
    combination)
2 zucchini, sliced
1 cup peas, fresh or frozen
salt and pepper to taste
Parmesan cheese (optional)

In a large soup pot, melt butter; add onion, celery, and carrots. Cook, stirring occasionally, until onion is soft and translucent. Add the potato, tomatoes, broth, and basil. Bring to a boil and then reduce heat, cover, and simmer for 15 minutes.

Add the cauliflower or broccoli and zucchini and simmer, covered, for 10 minutes.

Add the peas and simmer until tender. (This won't take but a few minutes.)

Season to taste with salt and pepper, and serve. A bit of Parmesan cheese sprinkled on top of the soup adds a nice garnish if desired.

Notes:

59

49 White Bean Soup

1 lb. white beans (navy or great northern)
2½ quarts water—enough to completely cover the beans
1 ham hock
1 stalk celery, chunked into thirds
1 onion, diced
salt and pepper to taste

Place the beans in a large soup pot and add the water. Bring to a boil and then turn off the heat. Cover the pot and let sit for an hour. Drain water from the beans, refill the soup pot with fresh water, and return the beans to the stove. Once the mixture begins boiling, turn down the heat so the beans simmer. Now is the time to add the ham hock, celery, and onion. Simmer the beans, covered, for 2 or more hours, stirring occasionally, or until the beans are tender. Remove the ham hock and celery from the soup. Discard the celery, let the ham hock cool enough to take off any meat, and add the ham back into the pot. When ready to serve, salt and pepper to taste.

Our family loves this soup plain with cornbread on the side. But sometimes we like to eat it ladled over cooked rice with chopped tomatoes on top. Delicious!

Notes:

50 Zucchini Soup

If you garden, chances are you'll have a glut of zucchini at some point. Here's a good way to use some of that surplus.

1 T. butter
2 cups zucchini, thinly sliced
½ cup onion
1 tsp. lemon juice
2 cups chicken broth
1 cup heavy cream or half-and-half
salt and pepper to taste

In a soup pot, melt butter and then add the zucchini and onion and cook until the vegetables are tender, stirring gently but regularly. Add the lemon juice and chicken broth and bring to a simmer; cook, covered, for about 15 minutes. Reduce heat slightly and add the cream; heat until thoroughly hot. Add salt and pepper to taste, and serve.

You can enhance the flavor of this soup by adding a bit of garlic, dill weed, rosemary, or basil. We like a bit of garlic and dill weed.

Notes:

STEWS

A hearty stew is pure comfort food. And because stew mostly just simmers undisturbed until you're ready to serve, it's a boon to busy cooks who don't have time to fuss in the kitchen preparing a meal. Simply cut up some meat and vegetables, add liquid and seasonings, and you're good to go.

Pot Roast with Carrots and Potatoes is a classic dish for good reason—who doesn't love meat and potatoes swimming in delicious gravy? For a change of pace, try the Black Beans with Pork and Citrus Sauce or the Apple Cider Pork Stew with Cheese Dumplings. The Five-Hour Beef Stew is perfect for lunch after church on Sunday because it slow cooks in the oven while you're away. Stonaflesch is an old-fashioned dry stew with few ingredients that is big on taste—and kids love it.

Stew doesn't have to be the same old thing. There are 49 recipes in this section for you to try. I'm sure you'll find some new favorites here. So get cooking and enjoy!

Everything that lives and moves about will be food for you.
Just as I gave you the green plants, I now give you everything.

GENESIS 9:3

- - - - - - - - - -

*Father, You are so generous to us! You made the
earth abundant with many good things, and all
for our benefit. Help me today to be mindful of
Your bounty as I make the food that my loved ones
will eat. And as I work in the kitchen, remind
me to use this time to pray for my family and the
needs of others. Bring to mind the sister who is
struggling with grief or depression, the brother
who has a family to provide for and is out of work
or injured, or the nation that is on the brink of
disaster. Open the eyes of my heart, that I might
see and respond to those around me who could
use some support or encouragement. And open
my hands wide, Lord, that I might be generous
in giving according to Your will. Amen.*

51 Apple Cider Pork Stew with Cheese Dumplings

For stew:
3 T. flour
1 tsp. salt
¼ tsp. thyme
⅛ tsp. pepper
¾ lb. boneless pork loin (chops or roast), cubed
2 T. oil
2 cups apple cider or apple juice
1 cup water
3 cups sweet potatoes, peeled and cubed (about 3 sweet potatoes)
2 cups apples, peeled or unpeeled (cook's choice), seeded, and cubed (about 2 apples)
1 cup onion, chopped
2 T. water

For cheese dumplings:
1 cup flour
1½ tsp. baking powder
¼ tsp. salt
⅔ cup buttermilk
¼ cup Cheddar cheese
½ tsp. parsley flakes (optional)

To make stew: In a medium mixing bowl or gallon-sized plastic bag, mix together the flour, salt, thyme, and pepper. Add the pork cubes and stir or shake to coat pork evenly. Place coated pork cubes on waxed paper and reserve remaining flour mixture to be used a bit later.

Notes:

In a Dutch oven or large saucepan, heat oil over medium-high heat; add pork cubes and cook, stirring occasionally, for about 5 minutes or until browned on all sides. Add all remaining stew ingredients except for the reserved flour and 2 tablespoons water. Bring to a boil; reduce heat, cover, and simmer 45-60 minutes or until pork is tender, stirring occasionally.

In a small bowl, mix together the reserved flour mixture and 2 tablespoons water and blend until smooth. Add to the stew; cook and stir for several minutes until stew is slightly thickened.

To make cheese dumplings: Mix together the flour, baking powder, and salt. Add the buttermilk, cheese, and parsley (if using) and stir just until moistened. Drop by tablespoonfuls into hot stew. Cover Dutch oven tightly and cook 25-35 minutes or until dumplings are fluffy and no longer doughy. Don't peek sooner than 25 minutes.

Notes:

52 Bean Stew

1½ cups dried beans (black, small red, or pinto beans are great
    in this recipe)
2 T. olive oil
1-2 onions, chopped
½ cup carrots, peeled and sliced or chopped
½ cup celery, sliced
½ cup green or red bell pepper, seeded and chopped
5-6 cups beef, chicken, or vegetable broth, divided
2 T. garlic, minced
2 cups fresh tomatoes, skinned and chopped, or 1 14½-ounce
    can diced tomatoes, undrained
2 T. tomato paste
2 T. honey
2-4 tsp. chili powder
1-2 tsp. cumin
½ tsp. oregano
splash of lemon or lime juice (optional)
shredded cheese, sour cream, fresh snipped cilantro or parsley
    for garnishes

Soak the beans in water overnight. Or, if you want to make the stew today, you can put the dried beans in a large stockpot, cover with water, and bring the mixture to a boil; cover the pot, turn off heat, and let the beans sit for an hour. Both of these methods help the beans to soften and cook more evenly and quickly. Whichever method you use, when the time is up, drain and rinse the beans and set them aside.

In a large stockpot, heat the olive oil along with a splash of the broth; add the onions, carrots, celery, and bell pepper and cook until the vegetables are limp. Add the garlic and continue to cook, stirring gently, for 1 minute. Add the beans, 4 cups of the remaining broth, tomatoes,

Notes:

tomato paste, honey, chili powder, cumin, and oregano to the pot; cover and simmer until beans are cooked, about 1½ -2 hours. (Variables such as how old and dry the beans are, how long they soaked, and what variety you use make this timing approximate only.) Add more broth if needed during the cooking process. When beans are thoroughly cooked, add a splash of lemon or lime juice if desired. (I think it helps to brighten the flavors, so I usually add some.)

Ladle into individual bowls and serve with garnishes of your choice.

Note: You can save time by using 3 cans of store-bought or home-canned pint jars of beans instead of using dried beans. Drain and rinse the beans, and then follow the instructions beginning with the second paragraph.

STEWS

Notes:

53 Beef and Sweet Potato Stew

2 lbs. beef stew meat, cubed
¼ cup flour
3 T. oil
2 onions, chopped
4 cloves garlic, minced
4 cups beef broth
2 sweet potatoes, peeled and chopped
4 carrots, peeled and sliced
2 bay leaves
1 tsp. thyme
salt and pepper to taste

Dredge the beef cubes in the flour to coat the meat thoroughly, either by stirring in a mixing bowl or shaking the beef and flour in a gallon-sized plastic bag. Remove the meat and discard the extra flour.

Heat the oil in a heavy stockpot or Dutch oven; add meat and brown on all sides. (You may have to work in batches. If so, you may need a bit more oil.) With a slotted spoon, remove the meat and set aside for now. Add the onions and garlic and cook until the onions are limp. Add remaining ingredients and simmer for about 1-1½ hours. Keep the simmer as low as possible and stir occasionally. If it seems as though the broth is evaporating more than you want, cover the pot with a tight-fitting lid, reduce the heat a bit more, and continue cooking until done.

Notes:

54 Beef and Turnip Stew

¾ lb. beef (bottom round, eye round, or chuck steak), cubed
2 tsp. olive oil
1 tsp. rosemary (2 tsp. if fresh)
2 onions, sliced
3 cloves garlic, minced
2½ cups beef broth
1 T. tomato paste
¼ tsp. pepper
6 turnips, cleaned and cut into ½-inch cubes
4 carrots, peeled and sliced

STEWS

Brown beef cubes in olive oil. When meat has been browned on all sides, add the rosemary, onions, and garlic and cook for 2 to 3 minutes, stirring constantly. Stir in broth, tomato paste, and pepper. Cover and cook for 45 minutes or until meat is thoroughly cooked and tender.

Add the turnips and carrots and cook about 20 minutes or until the vegetables are tender, stirring occasionally.

Notes:

55 Beef Stew with Coffee

1 cup flour
1½ tsp. salt
½ tsp. pepper
1 tsp. thyme
3 lbs. stew beef, cubed
3 T. oil
5 cups beef broth
1 cup strong brewed coffee
1 T. Worcestershire sauce
1 tsp. paprika
1 tsp. sugar
3 T. catsup
6 potatoes, peeled and quartered
2 small or 1 large onion, quartered
6 carrots, peeled and quartered
½ cup peas, fresh or frozen

Place the flour, salt, pepper, and thyme in a medium-sized mixing bowl or gallon-sized plastic bag and mix or shake to blend. Add the beef cubes, working in batches, and shake or stir to coat. You can set the coated pieces on a cookie sheet as you continue coating all the beef cubes.

In a large stockpot, heat the oil and add the beef cubes; brown on all sides. (You may need to add a bit more oil, especially if you brown the beef in batches.) Next, add all remaining ingredients, except for the peas, and simmer, covered, for about 1½-2 hours. Add the peas and continue to simmer the stew until peas are done, about 10-15 minutes more.

Note: When I know I'm going to be making this stew for lunch or dinner, I purposely make extra coffee in the morning. I measure out a cup and put it in the fridge (covered) until time to make the stew.

Notes:

71

56 Beef Stew with Dumplings

For stew:
3 T. shortening, lard, or oil
2 lbs. beef stew meat, cubed
2 T. flour
1½ tsp. salt
⅛ tsp. pepper
1 quart boiling water
1 tsp. lemon juice

For dumplings:
1 cup flour
1½ tsp. baking powder
½ tsp. salt
1 egg
2-3 T. milk
1 T. butter or shortening, melted and cooled slightly

To make stew: Melt shortening in a Dutch oven or large, deep skillet with a lid. Add the meat cubes and brown well on all sides. Sprinkle flour, salt, and pepper over the meat; add the boiling water and lemon juice and then cover the pot, lower the heat, and simmer for about 3 hours. Check occasionally to see if additional water is needed.

To make dumplings: In a medium-sized mixing bowl, stir together the flour, baking powder, and salt. In another bowl, mix together the egg, milk, and melted butter. Make a well in the center of the dry ingredients and pour the egg mixture into the well. Mix just until incorporated—you don't want to overmix the dough. Drop dough by large spoonfuls into simmering stew; cover the pot and allow the dumplings to cook without raising the lid for 15 minutes. (You might need a bit more cooking time, especially if the dumplings are on the large side, but it's better to have smaller and more dumplings than large ones.)

Notes:

57 Black Beans with Pork and Citrus Sauce

For stew:
2 T. olive oil
½-1 lb. pork, cubed
2 cloves garlic, minced
1 small onion, chopped
1 large or 2 medium tomatoes, skinned and chopped
salt and pepper to taste
3 15-ounce cans black beans, rinsed and drained (you can use pintos if you prefer)
beef broth or water as needed (at least a quart)
hot cooked rice for serving

For citrus sauce:
⅓ cup lemon juice
⅓ cup orange juice
½ tsp. cumin
1 tsp. basil
1 tsp. oregano
2 cloves garlic, minced

To make the stew: In a large pot, heat the oil and add the pork. Brown all sides and then add the garlic, onion, tomatoes, rinsed beans, and enough broth or water to barely cover. Cover the pot with a lid and cook on low heat for several hours so the stew has a chance to thicken a bit. (Although you can eat it much sooner than that, say, after an hour of cook time.)

To make citrus sauce: Mix together all the ingredients in a jar with a tight-fitting lid. Shake hard. Sometimes the spices want to float on top

Notes:

and the minced garlic likes to drop to the bottom, so I usually take a spoon and mix and scoop when I'm ready to use it.

To serve, place some hot cooked rice in the bottom of individual bowls. Add the stew and then spoon some citrus sauce on top. Don't be shy with the sauce because it's delicious!

- -

58 Buffet Beef Cubes with Noodles

STEWS

1½ lbs. beef chuck, trimmed of fat and cubed
2 T. flour
2 T. shortening
2¼ cups V-8 juice
¼ cup water
1 T. sugar
1½ tsp. salt
½ tsp. basil
¼ tsp. pepper
1 T. Worcestershire sauce
1 tsp. white vinegar
1½ cups onion, diced
1 bay leaf
3 cups uncooked egg noodles

In a gallon-sized plastic bag, add the meat cubes and flour and shake well to coat the meat.

In a heavy stewpot (enamel-coated cast iron works well for this recipe), melt the shortening and then add the meat; brown on all sides. Mix together the remaining ingredients, except the uncooked noodles, and simmer, covered, for about 2 hours or until the beef is tender and the sauce is thick like gravy. Stir often to prevent sticking.

Notes:

When close to mealtime, cook the egg noodles in enough water to cover (boil them according to the package directions); drain noodles and add to the stew or put some noodles on serving dishes and ladle the stew over the top.

Note: Egg noodles don't expand nearly as much as regular pasta such as spaghetti noodles. I get a little more than 4 cups of cooked noodles from 3 cups of uncooked. Yours might differ, so you may need to experiment with the amount of noodles you cook. Also, some people like more noodles and others prefer less.

59 Chicken Alfredo Stew

STEWS

4 T. butter
4 T. flour
2 cups milk
    Or
1 jar (16 ounces) Alfredo pasta sauce
¾ cup water
1 tsp. dried basil leaves if making homemade Alfredo, or ½ tsp. if using store-bought
½ tsp. salt
2 T. oil
1¼ lbs. boneless, skinless chicken thighs, chunked
4 cups potatoes, peeled and diced
1 cup carrots, peeled and diced
½ cup corn, fresh or frozen
½ cup peas, fresh or frozen
Parmesan cheese for serving

If making homemade Alfredo sauce: Melt butter in a medium saucepan; add flour while stirring constantly. Continuing to stir constantly,

Notes:

gradually add the milk and keep stirring until mixture begins to bubble and thicken. Add the water, basil leaves, and salt and stir to mix well. Taste and adjust seasonings; you might need a bit more salt and you can add some pepper if you desire.

To make stew: In a large pot, heat the oil; add the chicken pieces and brown lightly on all sides. Add the homemade Alfredo sauce, or, if you are using the store-bought sauce, add that to the pot along with water, basil, and salt. Stir to mix. Next, add the potatoes and carrots and bring to a slow simmer; cover the pot and cook the stew until the potatoes and carrots are tender and the chicken is cooked thoroughly, about 20-25 minutes. Add the corn and peas and cook for about 5-10 minutes longer or until done. Serve with Parmesan cheese to taste.

60 Chicken and Lentil Stew

4 cups chicken broth
½ cup lentils
½ cup pearl barley
1 cup cooked chicken, cubed
½ cup carrots, peeled and chopped or sliced
½ cup celery, diced
¼ cup onion, diced
salt, pepper, and dehydrated parsley to taste

Pour broth into a pot, add the lentils and barley, and simmer, covered, for 1 hour. Add the remaining ingredients and simmer for at least another 30 minutes, or until barley, lentils, and vegetables are tender. Add more broth or water if stew starts looking too dry.

Notes:

61 Chicken Goulash

1 whole chicken
2 cups tomatoes, chopped
2 tsp. salt
3 onions, chopped
1 green bell pepper, seeded and chopped
4 potatoes, peeled and cubed
1-2 T. paprika
sour cream (optional)

Boil the chicken in water to cover until tender, about 2½ hours. Remove chicken from the broth so both can cool faster. When cool, remove the meat from the skin and bones and cut the meat into bite-sized pieces; strain off as much fat from the broth as you can.

Return the meat to the strained broth, add remaining ingredients except for the sour cream, and simmer for 1 hour. Taste and adjust seasonings as desired.

To serve, ladle into individual bowls and top each with a dollop of sour cream.

STEWS

Notes:

62 Chicken Stew

2 T. oil

2-3 lbs. boneless, skinless chicken thighs or breasts, cubed

3 potatoes, peeled and chunked (or use 5 red potatoes and leave skins on)

2 cups carrots, peeled and thickly sliced

1 cup button mushrooms, sliced

½ cup onion

½ tsp. salt

¼ tsp. garlic powder

2¼ cups chicken gravy (or use 1½ jars [12 ounces each] of store-bought chicken gravy)

1 T. tomato paste

½ cup water or chicken broth

parsley for garnish (fresh or dehydrated)

In a large Dutch oven or pot, heat oil; add chicken pieces and brown on all sides. Add remaining ingredients except for parsley, cover pot, and cook on a low simmer until chicken is done and vegetables are tender, about 45 minutes.

To serve, ladle into individual bowls and garnish with a bit of parsley.

Notes:

63 Chicken, Sweet Potato, and Cabbage Stew

3 cups sweet potatoes, peeled and cubed
2 T. olive oil
1½ lbs. boneless, skinless chicken breasts, cubed
3 cups chicken broth
3 cups cabbage, coarsely shredded
1 can baby lima beans or butter beans, drained (cans are usually
    around 16 ounces, depending on which kind you buy)
1 14½-ounce can diced tomatoes, undrained
1 cup celery, sliced
1 cup tomato juice
salt and pepper to taste

In a saucepan, place cubed sweet potatoes and cover with water; bring to a boil, reduce heat, and simmer until sweet potatoes are almost tender. Drain sweet potatoes and set aside for now.

In a stockpot, heat the olive oil and brown the pieces of chicken on all sides. Add the chicken broth and half-cooked sweet potato cubes and bring to a boil; reduce heat, add the remaining ingredients, and simmer until the chicken is thoroughly cooked and the sweet potatoes are tender.

Notes:

64 Chili Verde

2 T. oil
¾ lb. beef chuck or round roast, cubed
¾ lb. boneless pork shoulder roast, cubed
5 cloves garlic, minced
2 28-ounce cans tomatoes, cut up (or 4 14½-ounce cans diced tomatoes)
8 4-ounce cans diced green chilies, drained
1 green bell pepper, chopped
1 cup beef broth
2 tsp. ground cumin
½ tsp. sugar
¼ tsp. ground cloves
3 jalapeño peppers, seeded and chopped (optional)
⅓ cup fresh parsley, snipped

Heat oil in a large Dutch oven or heavy pot; brown the meat half at a time, adding garlic to the second half of the browning. Drain off excess fat and return all meat to the Dutch oven. Add remaining ingredients except for the parsley. Bring to a boil and then turn down the heat, cover the pot, and simmer for 2 hours, stirring occasionally. Uncover and simmer for another 30 minutes or so until desired consistency. Stir in parsley just before serving.

Notes:

65 Chili with Beans

2 lbs. hamburger
1 onion (or 2 smaller onions), chopped
1 green bell pepper, chopped
3-4 cloves garlic, minced
2 T. chili powder
2 tsp. cumin
2 tsp. coriander
1 tsp. oregano
1 tsp. red pepper flakes (optional)
2 15-ounce cans kidney or pinto beans, or 2 quarts home-
    canned beans
2 15-ounce cans tomato sauce
2 14½-ounce cans diced tomatoes, undrained
salt and pepper to taste

In a Dutch oven or heavy pot, brown the hamburger just until the meat is no longer pink; drain grease. Add the onion, bell pepper, garlic, chili powder, cumin, coriander, oregano, and pepper flakes and continue to brown the meat, stirring regularly, for another several minutes. Next, add the beans, tomato sauce, and diced tomatoes and bring to a gentle boil. Reduce heat, cover the pot, and simmer for about 1 hour. Remove the cover and continue to simmer for about 30 more minutes, or until the chili has thickened a bit and has a deep color. (If the sauce cooks down too quickly, you can add some water, about ½ cup at a time, so the chili doesn't stick to the bottom of the pot.

Ladle into individual serving bowls and, if desired, top with shredded Cheddar or Jack cheese, sour cream, diced avocados, or sliced green onions.

Notes:

66 Chili Without Beans

1½ lbs. hamburger
2 14½-ounce cans diced or stewed tomatoes, undrained
1 8-ounce can tomato sauce
1 small onion, chopped
1 green bell pepper, chopped
1 4-ounce can chopped green chilies
1 T. chili powder
2 cloves garlic, minced
1 tsp. salt
½ tsp. paprika
¼ tsp. pepper
½ cup fresh minced parsley

In a heavy pot, brown hamburger; drain grease. Add the remainder of the ingredients except for the parsley. Simmer for about an hour; add the parsley and simmer for 10 minutes more.

Ladle into individual bowls and serve. Or top with shredded cheese (Jack, Cheddar, or crumbled Cotija), a dollop of sour cream, and sliced green onions if desired. Some people like to serve this over cooked rice.

Notes:

67 Chilly Day Stew

2 carrots, peeled and sliced
2 cups water
1 large or 2 small onions, diced
4 cups potatoes, peeled and cubed
2 T. uncooked white rice
⅓ cup uncooked elbow macaroni
1 tsp. salt
½ tsp. pepper
2 cups milk
2 T. butter

Add carrots and water to a large pot; bring to a boil, reduce heat, and simmer until carrots are almost tender, about 15 minutes. Add the onions, potatoes, rice, macaroni, salt, and pepper and bring to a boil once again; reduce heat and simmer until rice is cooked and vegetables are tender, about 30 minutes more. (Add more water only if absolutely necessary.)

Add the milk and butter and stir; heat until hot, but do not boil.

Note: You can substitute 2 cups heavy cream for the milk and butter if you prefer.

Notes:

68 Classic Beef Stew

1½ lbs. beef stew meat, cubed
¼ cup flour
1-2 T. oil
5 carrots, peeled and thickly sliced
4 potatoes, peeled and chunked
1 onion, chunked
2 cups beef or vegetable broth
1 cup water
2 tsp. salt
2 tsp. pepper
2 large bay leaves
½ tsp. thyme
¼ cup flour (optional)
¼ cup water (optional)

Dredge the meat cubes in the flour. In a heavy pot or cast-iron Dutch oven, heat the oil and then add the flour-coated meat cubes and brown on all sides. Add the carrots, potatoes, onion, broth, 1 cup water, salt, pepper, bay leaves, and thyme. Cover with a tight-fitting lid and bake in the oven at 300° for 3-4 hours.

Optional: If you like your stew thicker, mix together ¼ cup of flour with ¼ cup water and stir it into the stew before cooking.

Before serving, remove the bay leaves and discard. Taste and adjust seasonings as desired. (You may need more salt.)

Notes:

69 Colorful Beef Stew

¼ cup flour
1 tsp. garlic powder
3 tsp. mustard powder
1 tsp. chili powder
¼ tsp. pepper
1 lb. beef stew meat, cubed into bite-sized pieces
2 T. oil
1 14½-ounce can diced tomatoes, undrained
2 cups beef broth (or use 1 14½-ounce can)
1 tsp. Worcestershire sauce
3 carrots, peeled and thickly sliced
2 small or 1 large onion, chunked
1½ cups zucchini, chunked
1½ cups corn, fresh or frozen
⅓ cup water

In a mixing bowl or gallon-sized plastic bag, mix together the flour, garlic powder, mustard powder, chili powder, and pepper. Add beef cubes and stir or shake to evenly coat pieces of meat. Save any remaining flour mixture to be used a bit later.

In a Dutch oven or large, heavy-bottomed pot, heat oil until hot. Add the beef cubes and cook for about 5 minutes, or until cubes are evenly browned on all sides, stirring occasionally. Add the tomatoes, broth, Worcestershire sauce, carrots, and onions. Bring to a boil and then reduce heat to maintain a low simmer. Cover and cook for 1-1½ hours or until beef is tender, stirring occasionally.

Stir in zucchini and corn and continue to simmer, covered, for another 15-20 minutes.

In a small bowl, blend together the reserved flour mixture and water until smooth. Add to stew and cook, stirring for several minutes or until the stew has thickened.

Notes:

70 Creamy Beef Stew

2 T. oil
1½ lbs. beef stew meat, cubed
2 cups beef broth
1 clove garlic, minced
1 T. paprika
3 leeks
1 green or red bell pepper
½ lb. small button mushrooms
1 T. cornstarch
2 T. apple juice
¼ cup heavy whipping cream
salt and pepper to taste

In a large Dutch oven or stockpot, heat oil; add meat cubes and brown on all sides. Stir in broth, minced garlic, and paprika. Bring to a boil and then cover the pot, reduce heat, and simmer until the meat is thoroughly cooked and tender, about 1 hour.

To prepare leeks, cut off and discard the tops and very dark green portion. Cut the leeks lengthwise so you can rinse them well and then slice them thickly. Cut and seed the bell pepper and chop coarsely. Scrub the mushrooms to get off all dirt. If they are very small, you can leave them whole; if not, halve or thickly slice them.

Add the vegetables to the stew, bring to a boil, and then cover the pot, reduce the heat, and simmer until vegetables are tender, about 20 minutes.

Mix together the cornstarch and apple juice. Add to the cream and stir to mix. After the vegetables are tender, increase the heat, add the cream mixture while stirring constantly, and keep stirring until the mixture thickens. Add salt and pepper to taste.

We like this served over cooked rice, but it's good plain as well.

Notes:

71 Creamy Chicken Stew

2 T. oil
3 lbs. boneless, skinless chicken breasts, cubed
1 tsp. salt
1 tsp. pepper
1 tsp. paprika
2 cups potatoes, peeled and cubed
3 carrots, peeled and thickly sliced
2 cups corn, fresh or frozen
1 cup green bell pepper, coarsely chopped
1 cup red bell pepper, coarsely chopped
1 cup celery, thickly sliced
1 onion, chopped
2 tsp. basil
1 bay leaf
¼ tsp. celery salt
7 cups chicken broth, divided
¼ cup butter
¾ cup flour

Heat oil and cook the chicken, salt, pepper, and paprika until chicken is done, stirring occasionally. Add the vegetables, basil, bay leaf, celery salt, and 5 cups of the broth. Bring to a boil and then reduce heat, cover the pot, and simmer 20 minutes or until the potatoes and carrots are tender. Remove bay leaf.

In a medium saucepan, melt the butter and stir in the flour, stirring constantly. Gradually add 2 cups broth, stirring constantly until thickened. Pour this roux back into the pot with the stew and stir to mix. Bring to a boil, reduce heat, and simmer uncovered until hot, about 5 minutes.

STEWS

Notes:

72 Creamy Potato and Vegetable Stew

3 quarts water
8 large potatoes, peeled and cubed
4-6 carrots, peeled and sliced or chopped
2 stalks celery, sliced
⅓ cup butter
2 small or 1 large onion, chopped
2 T. flour
1½ tsp. salt
1 tsp. pepper
¼ tsp. paprika
2 cups heavy cream

In a large pot or Dutch oven, add the water, potatoes, carrots, and celery and bring to a boil. Decrease heat and simmer until the vegetables are just barely tender. Drain the vegetables and set them aside, reserving the liquid in a separate bowl.

In the same pot, melt the butter; add the onions and cook slowly for 10 minutes, stirring often, or until the onions are very tender. Add the flour, salt, pepper, and paprika and stir; gradually add the cream while stirring constantly. Continue stirring for several minutes so the flour doesn't lump. Add the vegetables back into the pot and add the reserved liquid, a spoonful at a time to get the desired consistency.

Ladle into individual serving bowls. If desired, sprinkle on a small amount of fresh snipped parsley, a shake of paprika, or diced fresh tomatoes.

Notes:

73 Easy Hamburger Stew

½-1 lb. hamburger
1 small onion, chopped
1 quart home-canned green beans (or you can use a quart of
    fresh green beans, cut in 1-inch pieces)
6 potatoes, peeled and cubed
2 quarts beef broth
salt and pepper to taste
summer savory and/or thyme to taste (optional)

Brown the hamburger; drain off the fat. Add the rest of the ingredients and simmer until potatoes are tender.

Note: I usually use canned green beans, and when I do, I make sure the potatoes are cut into smaller bite-sized pieces so the stew cooks quicker since the canned green beans are already thoroughly cooked.

Notes:

74 Elk Stew

2 T. oil
2 lbs. elk stew meat, cubed
flour for dredging meat
1 quart water
2 cups beef broth
1 bay leaf
6 carrots, peeled and sliced
5 potatoes, peeled and cubed
1 onion, chopped
1 can cream of mushroom soup
½ cup flour mixed with 1 cup water
salt and pepper to taste

STEWS

Heat oil in a heavy pot or Dutch oven. Dredge elk meat in flour, sprinkle the pieces of meat with a bit of salt and pepper, and brown on all sides. Add 1 quart water, broth, and bay leaf and simmer for 1 hour.

Add the carrots, potatoes, onion, and soup; simmer for 30 more minutes.

Gradually pour the flour and water mixture into the stew, stirring constantly until the stew has thickened. Add more salt and pepper if needed. Remove bay leaf and serve.

Note: You can add more broth or water for a saucier stew or if too much liquid evaporates while simmering.

Notes:

75 Five-Hour Beef Stew

2 lbs. beef stew meat, cubed
3 potatoes, peeled and chunked
3 chopped onions
6 carrots, peeled and thickly sliced
1 cup celery, sliced
1 quart canned tomatoes (or you can use 1½ cans [14½ ounces each] stewed tomatoes)
3 T. minute tapioca
½ T. sugar
1 T. salt
1 slice stale bread, torn into bite-sized pieces

Mix all ingredients together in a Dutch oven or large glass baking dish. Cover tightly. (If using the baking dish, use a double layer of foil to tightly cover the stew.) Bake at 250º for 5 hours. (If using the baking dish, check after about 4 hours to make sure it isn't cooking too fast. You don't even need to open the foil cover. Just peek around the edges to make sure it's not too dark looking.)

STEWS

Notes:

76 Gibson Stew

STEWS

2 lbs. round steak, cubed
3 cups water
1 tsp. salt
½ tsp. pepper
1 onion, chopped
3 stalks celery, sliced
4 carrots, peeled and sliced
4 potatoes, peeled and chopped
1 turnip, peeled and chopped
1 15-ounce can peas, drained
1 15-ounce can corn, drained
1 14½-ounce can diced tomatoes, undrained
¼ cup flour
¼ cup water

In a heavy stewpot, brown the meat; add 3 cups water, salt, and pepper and cook on fairly low heat, covered, for 30-40 minutes. Add the onion, celery, and carrots and cook for 15 minutes. Now add the potatoes and turnip and cook, covered, for about 45 minutes, adding more water if needed. Add the cans of peas, corn, and tomatoes and cook until thoroughly heated through.

Make a mixture of flour and ¼ cup water by shaking or whisking it until smooth; add to the stew and cook, stirring until stew thickens. Serve.

Notes:

77 Ground Turkey Chili

2 tsp. oil
1 onion, chopped
3 carrots, peeled and sliced or chopped
1 green bell pepper, seeded and chopped
1 cup fresh mushrooms, sliced
1 lb. ground turkey
2 tsp. oregano
1-2 T. chili powder
1 tsp. cumin
pepper to taste
2 28-ounce cans crushed tomatoes
1 tsp. hot red pepper sauce (i.e., Tabasco, Cholula, or Sriracha)
6 cloves garlic, minced
1 quart home-canned red beans (or 2 15-ounce cans kidney or
    small red beans), drained

In a large stewpot, sauté onion, carrots, and bell pepper in oil for 3 minutes; add the mushrooms and cook 3 minutes more. Add the turkey, oregano, chili powder, cumin, and pepper and cook, breaking up ground turkey, until meat is no longer pink. Add the remaining ingredients, stir well, and simmer over low heat for 30-45 minutes, stirring occasionally.

You can garnish individual bowls of stew with shredded cheese, a dollop of sour cream, and some fresh parsley or cilantro if desired.

Notes:

78 I-Can't-Cook Stew

1 lb. hamburger
2 cans vegetable soup
1 can water or beef broth (use 1½-2 cans of water if the soup
    you are using is condensed)
2 cans ranch-style beans, undrained

In a stewpot, brown the hamburger; drain off fat. Add the remaining ingredients and simmer until hamburger is cooked through.

Seriously. Don't you have those days when you need to feed the family and don't have the time or the inclination to make a meal? This will take care of those days nicely. Butter some bread and call it dinner.

STEWS

79 Just Pork Stew

3 T. oil
3 lbs. boneless pork roast, cubed
1 onion, thin sliced
3 T. soy sauce
¼ cup cider vinegar
1 clove garlic, minced
2 bay leaves
1 cup plus 1 T. water, divided
2 tsp. cornstarch
hot cooked rice
green onions, sliced

Heat oven to 450º. Pour the oil into a large ovenproof roaster about 9 x 13 inches and place in the oven to get hot during preheating. When

Notes:

the oil is hot, add the meat and onion and bake, uncovered, for about 15-20 minutes or until meat is browned; reduce heat to 350º.

In a small bowl, mix together the soy sauce, vinegar, garlic, bay leaves, and 1 cup of the water. Pour onto the meat. Cover the roaster and bake for 30 minutes more or until the meat is cooked through and tender. With a slotted spoon, remove the meat to another dish and keep warm.

Pour drippings from the roaster into a saucepan, remove bay leaves, and allow drippings to sit undisturbed for several minutes to give the fat time to rise to the top. Skim off as much as you can. Turn on heat, bring drippings to a boil and boil until liquid has been reduced to 1 cup. (Just eyeball it—no need to measure.)

Mix together the cornstarch and 1 T. water and pour it into the drippings, stirring constantly. Continue to stir constantly until the mixture thickens. Pour over the meat and gently mix to coat all pieces.

To serve, spoon some hot cooked rice onto plates or into bowls, ladle pork on top of rice, and sprinkle with green onions.

Notes:

80 Lamb Stew

1½ lbs. lamb stew meat, cubed
2 T. olive oil, divided
3 onions, quartered
4 carrots, peeled and thickly sliced
5 potatoes, peeled and cubed
2 cups beef broth
1 tsp. salt
¼ tsp. pepper
1 T. butter
1 T. flour
½ tsp. parsley
½ tsp. thyme

Preheat oven to 350º.

In a Dutch oven or heavy, ovenproof pot, brown the lamb cubes in 1 tablespoon of the olive oil until meat is browned on all sides; remove meat with slotted spoon and set aside. Add the remaining oil to the pot along with the onions and carrots and cook, stirring occasionally, for 5 minutes or until onions are tender and translucent. Add the potatoes, broth, salt, pepper, and browned lamb cubes. Bring to a boil and then cover the pot and put in the preheated oven. Bake for 50-60 minutes until the meat and vegetables are tender. Remove the meat and vegetables with a slotted spoon and set them aside and keep warm. Pour the pan juices into another bowl and set aside also.

In the Dutch oven, melt butter; stir in flour and keep stirring until smooth. Gradually stir in the reserved pan juices. Continuing to stir constantly, bring the mixture to a boil and simmer until thickened, about 2-3 minutes. Stir in the meat and vegetables, parsley, and thyme and heat thoroughly.

Notes:

81 Lentil and Sweet Potato Stew

1¼ cups lentils
6 cups chicken or vegetable broth
1 onion, quartered
2 cloves garlic, minced
1 bay leaf
½ tsp. turmeric
½ tsp. ground cumin
½ tsp. ginger
1 tsp. dried parsley
2 carrots, peeled and sliced
2 sweet potatoes, peeled and cubed
2 T. tomato paste

Rinse and drain lentils, picking out any debris as you do so. Put in a stockpot and add the remaining ingredients. Bring to a boil; reduce heat and simmer until the lentils are cooked and the sweet potatoes are tender. If the stew starts to get too dry, cover with a lid to finish cooking.

Notes:

82 Lentil Stew

2 cups lentils
6-7 cups beef broth
2 14½-ounce cans diced tomatoes, undrained
2 cups potatoes, peeled and cubed
1 cup carrots, peeled and sliced or chopped
1 cup onion, chopped
½ cup celery
2 cloves garlic, minced
1 T. Worcestershire sauce
1 T. dried parsley
1 T. dried basil
1 tsp. thyme
1 bay leaf
salt and pepper to taste

STEWS

Pick through lentils and then rinse and drain.

In a stockpot, combine lentils with 6 cups of the broth and the remaining ingredients. Simmer until lentils are tender, about 50-60 minutes. Stir occasionally and add more broth if the stew starts to look too dry. You can also cover the pot with a lid to reduce evaporation.

Before serving, remove bay leaf and discard.

Notes:

83 Lentil Stew with Ham and Swiss Chard

1½ T. oil
1 cup onion, chopped
3 cloves garlic, minced
5 cups chicken or vegetable broth
1 cup dried lentils, rinsed and drained
½ cup carrots, peeled and chopped
1½ cups potatoes, peeled and cubed
3 cups Swiss chard, chopped
2 bay leaves
1 cup cooked ham, cubed
1½ cups tomatoes, skinned and chopped
1 tsp. basil
½ tsp. thyme
½ tsp. pepper
snipped fresh parsley for garnish (optional)

Heat oil in a heavy stockpot; add the onion and garlic and sauté for several minutes or until the onion is limp and translucent. Add broth and lentils and bring to a boil; reduce heat, cover pot, and simmer for about 30 minutes.

Next, add carrots, potatoes, Swiss chard, and bay leaves. Bring to a boil again, and then reduce heat and simmer until the lentils and vegetables are tender, about 20 minutes.

Next, add the cooked ham, tomatoes, basil, thyme, and pepper; simmer for 10 minutes more. Discard bay leaves.

Ladle stew into individual bowls, sprinkle with parsley if using, and serve.

Note: I like to add the Swiss chard during the last few minutes of cooking so it retains a bit of crispness near the ribs. Cook's choice.

Notes:

84 Meatball Stew

1½ lbs. hamburger
1 egg, beaten
1 cup bread crumbs or 1 cup quick-cooking rolled oats
2 T. shortening or oil
1 onion, chunked
2-3 carrots, peeled and thickly sliced
4-5 potatoes, peeled and cubed
2 cans condensed tomato soup (10¾ ounces each)
2 soup cans water
1 quart beef broth (or use 2 14½-ounce cans)
¼ tsp. thyme

Use your hands to mix together the hamburger, egg, and bread crumbs. Roll into meatballs (the size isn't critical).

Melt shortening or heat oil in a stewpot and brown the meatballs; drain off excess grease. Add remaining ingredients and cook, gently stirring occasionally to prevent sticking. (Stirring too aggressively could cause meatballs to break apart.) Cook until vegetables are tender and meatballs are cooked thoroughly, about 1 hour.

Notes:

85 No-Peek Stew

1½ lbs. stew meat, cubed
5 potatoes, peeled and cubed
6 carrots, peeled and sliced
2 stalks celery, sliced
1 onion, sliced
1 green bell pepper, sliced
¼ cup mushrooms, sliced (or you can use a small can of sliced
    mushrooms, drained)
3 T. minute tapioca
1½ T. sugar
1 tsp. salt
¼ tsp. pepper
¼ tsp. garlic salt
1½ cups V-8 juice
1¼ cups peas (fresh or frozen)

Grease a large 10 x 13-inch baking dish. Put raw meat on the bottom of the baking dish. Then add in layers the potatoes, carrots, celery, onion, bell pepper, and mushrooms.

Mix together the minute tapioca, sugar, salt, pepper, and garlic salt and sprinkle over the meat and veggies. Pour V-8 juice over all, seal with a double layer of foil, and bake at 350º for 2-3 hours.

Place the peas in a medium saucepan, cover them with water, and bring them to a boil. Drain. Remove stew from oven and pour the peas on top of the stew just before serving.

Note: I usually use about 2 cups V-8 juice because we like the flavor and added moisture.

Notes:

86 Old-Fashioned Oyster Stew

2 pints raw shucked oysters, small to medium size
3 cups milk
2 cups cream
4 T. butter
salt and pepper to taste
Tabasco sauce to taste
sliced green onions and fresh snipped parsley for garnish

Drain oysters, reserving liquid but straining well to remove any debris or sand. Rinse oysters and check that they are clean.

In a large pot, heat together the milk, cream, and oyster liquid over medium-low heat. You want the mixture to be hot but not boiling.

In another large pot, melt butter. Add the oysters and simmer them gently, just until they begin to curl at the edges. This only takes a few minutes. (Don't overcook or the oysters will get tough and chewy.) Slowly pour in the heated milk mixture, stirring gently while adding. Taste the stew and add salt, pepper, and Tabasco sauce as desired.

Ladle into individual bowls and add a small pat of butter, sliced green onions, and fresh parsley. Serve with oyster crackers.

Notes:

87 One-Dish Meal

1 chicken (3-4 lbs.), cut into pieces
flour
salt and pepper
5 potatoes, peeled and thickly sliced
1 bunch green onions, sliced
1 can cream of mushroom soup
1 soup can water

Roll chicken pieces in flour that has been seasoned with salt and pepper and brown well on all sides, using a heavy-bottomed pot that can hold all the pieces at once.

Layer potatoes over the chicken and then the green onions on top of the potatoes.

Mix together the soup and water and pour over the top. Simmer slowly, covered, until chicken is cooked through and potatoes are tender, about 20-30 minutes.

You can serve this meal on plates, but large, shallow pasta bowls work well also.

STEWS

Notes:

88 Pot Roast with Carrots and Potatoes

1 T. oil
1 3-4 lbs. boneless chuck or round roast
4-6 potatoes, peeled and quartered
6-8 carrots, peeled and quartered
cornstarch
water
salt and pepper to taste

In a large stockpot or Dutch oven, heat oil; salt and pepper the roast and then place it in the pot and brown all sides. Fill the pot with enough water to barely cover the meat. Bring to a boil and then reduce heat, cover the pot, and simmer for about 3 hours. Add the potatoes and carrots, making sure they are submerged in the cooking liquid. Once again bring the contents to a boil and then reduce heat, cover the pot, and cook until the potatoes and carrots are tender.

Using a big slotted spoon, remove the meat, potatoes, and carrots from the pot and, keeping them separate, place them in heatproof dishes and set them aside and keep them warm. (I usually turn my oven on for a few minutes just to get the inside a bit warm and then turn off the heat and set my meat and veggies in the warm oven.)

Now to make the gravy: Keep the broth simmering in the Dutch oven. Estimate how many cups of broth you have in your pot, and for every cup of broth add 1 tablespoon cornstarch and 1 tablespoon water in a pourable mixing bowl or large liquid measuring cup and mix. This is called a cornstarch slurry. (I usually use a bit more water than cornstarch so it's a thinner slurry, but that's not necessary.) Slowly pour the slurry into the simmering broth, stirring constantly so the cornstarch doesn't clump. Stir constantly until the broth begins to

Notes:

bubble and thicken and the gravy becomes a bit clearer looking. Taste the gravy and add salt and pepper if needed.

To serve, put meat, carrots, and potatoes on individual plates and either pour gravy over everything, or bring the gravy to the table and let everyone pour their own.

89 Quick and Easy Taco Stew

1 lb. hamburger
1 medium onion, chunked
1 14- or 15-ounce can whole kernel corn, drained, or 2 cups
    fresh or frozen corn
1 14½-ounce can diced tomatoes with green chilies, undrained
1 16-ounce can pinto beans with chili sauce, undrained
1 10¾-ounce can condensed tomato soup, undiluted
1 cup water
tortilla chips and cheese for garnish

In a stewpot, brown the hamburger; drain off fat. Add remainder of ingredients and simmer for about 25-30 minutes or longer, making sure that the meat is thoroughly cooked before serving.

To serve, ladle into individual bowls and top with tortilla chips and cheese if desired.

Notes:

90 Rabbit Stew

1 rabbit, dressed and cut into pieces
2 cups water
flour for dredging
1 tsp. salt
¼ tsp. pepper
¼ cup oil
2 onions, sliced
2 cloves garlic, minced
½ cup vinegar
1 14½-15-ounce can stewed or diced tomatoes, undrained
1 6-ounce can tomato paste
½ tsp. ground cloves

Place the rabbit pieces in a stockpot and add the water; cover the pot and simmer until the meat is cooked thoroughly and beginning to fall off the bones. Remove the meat and set aside until cool enough to handle. While the meat is cooling, strain broth and save to add to the stew. Remove meat from bones and cut into large bite-sized pieces.

Roll pieces of meat in flour and sprinkle with salt and pepper. Heat the oil in a clean pot and fry the floured pieces of meat until browned on all sides. Using a slotted spoon, remove the meat and set aside. Add the onion slices to the same pot and cook until limp and lightly browned. Add back the meat and broth, and then add all other ingredients. Cover and let simmer for 1-1½ hours, or you can bake the stew in a covered, ovenproof pot at 350º for 1-1½ hours.

Notes:

91 Spicy Chicken Chili

2 T. oil
1¾ lbs. boneless, skinless chicken thighs or breasts, cut into
    large chunks
½ cup onion, chopped
2 stalks celery, sliced
2 14½-ounce cans diced tomatoes, undrained
1 quart pinto beans (or 2 15-ounce cans), drained
1½ cups enchilada sauce (1 10-ounce can)
2 tsp. chili powder
1 tsp. garlic, minced
1 tsp. cumin
corn chips, sour cream, shredded Cheddar cheese, juice from
    fresh limes, or chopped fresh cilantro for garnish (optional)

In a Dutch oven or large pot, heat the oil; add the chicken pieces and brown on all sides. Add the onion, celery, diced tomatoes, pinto beans, enchilada sauce, and spices, and stir to mix well. Cover pot and simmer gently until chicken is thoroughly cooked and tender.

When ready to serve, ladle chili into individual bowls and garnish with whatever sounds good and whatever you have on hand.

Notes:

92 Spicy Fish Stew

STEWS

1 T. oil
1 cup onion, chopped
¼ cup celery, sliced
1 tsp. chili powder
1½ cups corn, fresh or frozen
1 T. Worcestershire sauce
1 14½-ounce can diced tomatoes, undrained
2 cups water
1 lb. white fish such as rockfish, cod, tilapia, or halibut, cut into
    bite-sized pieces
cayenne pepper to taste
salt to taste
¼ cup chopped fresh cilantro or parsley

Heat oil in a pot; add onion, celery, and chili powder. Sauté until vegetables are tender.

Stir in corn, Worcestershire sauce, diced tomatoes, and water. Cook for 10 minutes. Add fish and cook until fish is done, about 3-5 minutes. Add cayenne pepper and salt to taste. Stir in cilantro and parsley.

Ladle into individual bowls and have some sliced lemons or limes on hand to squeeze juice over the stew if desired.

Notes:

93 Squirrel Stew

3 squirrels, dressed and cut into pieces
3 quarts water
¼ cup bacon, chopped
1 tsp. coriander or thyme
¼ tsp. cayenne pepper
2 tsp. salt
1 cup onions, chopped
4 tomatoes, skinned and chopped
2 cups potatoes, peeled and chopped
2 cups baby lima or butter beans (fresh is best, but you can use frozen)
2 cups corn (fresh is best, but you can use frozen)
¼ tsp. pepper

Place the squirrel pieces into a large pot and add water. Bring to a boil, reduce heat, and simmer for 1½-2 hours. Using a slotted spoon, remove squirrel and allow to cool enough so you can handle it. Remove meat from bones and return the meat to the pot. Add the bacon, coriander, cayenne pepper, salt, onions, tomatoes, potatoes, and lima beans, and simmer for 1 hour. Add the corn and cook 10 minutes longer. Add the pepper, adjust seasonings, and serve.

Notes:

94 Stonaflesch

2 lbs. hamburger
10 carrots, peeled and sliced
6 large potatoes, peeled and thinly sliced
salt and pepper
paprika

In a heavy ovenproof pot, layer a portion of the raw hamburger (break apart the hamburger into little pieces as you work) over the entire bottom. Next add a layer of carrots and then a layer of potatoes. Top each potato layer with salt and pepper and continue layering. It's better to have several thin layers than a few thick ones. Be sure to end with a small amount of hamburger as the top layer. Sprinkle paprika over the top and cover the pot with a tight-fitting lid.

Bake at 350° for at least an hour, or until carrots and potatoes are cooked through and tender. You can also cook the Stonaflesch at 250° for 3-4 hours, but you'll need to check occasionally to make sure the bottom doesn't scorch.

Note: This is a dry stew. In spite of its simplicity and very few ingredients, it's a soothing and tasty meal on a cold winter day.

Notes:

95 Swiss Steak

¼ cup flour
1 tsp. salt, divided
¼ tsp. pepper
2 lbs. round steak, cut into 1-inch-thick pieces
2 T. oil
¼ cup water
1 14½-ounce can diced tomatoes, undrained
1 large tomato, skinned and chopped
½ cup green bell pepper, diced
1 tsp. onion powder

Mix together the flour, ½ tsp. salt, and pepper. Sprinkle pieces of steak with flour mixture and pound the flour into the steak with something sturdy like a meat mallet or rolling pin.

In a large skillet, heat oil; add pieces of floured steak and brown on both sides. Don't hurry this process—take about 15-20 minutes to do the browning. Reduce heat to low, add the water, cover the skillet, and simmer until beef is tender, about 1 hour. Add more water as necessary to prevent the meat from scorching.

In a medium mixing bowl, stir together the diced tomatoes, chopped tomato, green bell pepper, onion powder, ½ tsp. salt, and a shake or two of pepper. Pour mixture over meat, bring to a simmer, and cook until sauce has thickened, about 30 minutes longer.

This is good with mashed potatoes, rice, or noodles.

Notes:

96 Three-Bean Meatless Chili

1 quart tomatoes, undrained (or 1 28-ounce can crushed
    tomatoes)
1 pint jar white beans, drained (or 1 15-ounce can, drained)
1 pint jar kidney beans, drained (or 1 15-ounce can, drained)
1 pint jar black beans, drained (or 1 15-ounce can, drained)
1 10-ounce can mild enchilada sauce
1 cup tomato sauce (½-pint jar or 8-ounce can)
1 4½-ounce can chopped mild green chilies
1 red bell pepper, seeded and diced
½ cup onion, diced
2-3 tsp. chili powder (depending on how spicy you like it)
1 tsp. oregano
½ tsp. cumin
Cheddar cheese, shredded

In a large pot, mix together all ingredients, except Cheddar cheese;
bring to a boil and then lower the heat, cover the pot, and simmer, stirring occasionally, for at least 30 minutes. An hour of cooking time is
best because it will better meld the ingredients.

To serve, ladle chili into individual bowls and top with Cheddar
cheese. A dollop of sour cream, chopped avocados, or broken tortilla
chips are tasty toppings too.

Notes:

97 Twenty-Four-Hour Beef Stew

3 lbs. beef stew meat, cubed

For marinade:
2 onions, thinly sliced
1 carrot, peeled and chopped
2 stalks celery, chunked
1 clove garlic, minced
1 tsp. salt
¼ tsp. thyme
2 bay leaves
¼ tsp. pepper
2 whole cloves
2 cups apple juice or cider
½ cup vegetable oil

For stew:
1 cup bacon pieces or cut-up salt pork
1 large onion, chunked
2 carrots, peeled and chopped
2 T. brown sugar
3 T. oil
3 T. flour
1 clove garlic, minced
⅔ cup apple juice or cider
2 stalks celery, sliced or chopped
4 sprigs parsley
1 bay leaf
¼ tsp. thyme
salt and pepper to taste
cooked rice for serving (optional)

Notes:

24 hours before: Place the cubed meat in a large baking dish. Mix together all marinade ingredients and pour over the meat, making sure that meat cubes are covered with marinade. Cover with plastic wrap and refrigerate for 24 hours.

After 24 hours, remove the meat from the marinade and pat dry on paper towels; strain and reserve the strained marinade.

To cook stew: In a Dutch oven or heavy pot, brown bacon and onion together. When lightly browned, add the carrots and sprinkle with brown sugar. Cook until the meat is completely browned; remove bacon and vegetables and set aside. Drain the bacon grease and use the same pan to continue.

Add oil and brown the stew meat. Sprinkle meat with flour and cook until the flour is golden. Add minced garlic, apple juice, celery, parsley sprigs, bay leaf, and thyme. Add reserved marinade and enough water to cover the meat. Add the bacon and vegetables; simmer, covered, 1½ hours, stirring occasionally and checking to be sure it doesn't get too dry. If there is too much liquid, remove the lid for the last 15-20 minutes.

Ladle into individual bowls and serve either as is or over some cooked rice.

Notes:

98 Venison Stew

4 T. olive oil
2-3 lbs. venison or elk steaks, rinsed, dried, and cubed
1 T. salt
pepper to taste
6 cups water
2 T. beef granules or 3 beef bouillon cubes
2 T. Worcestershire sauce
1 envelope dry onion soup mix
2 tsp. garlic, minced
4 potatoes, peeled and cubed (or use about 6 small red potatoes
   and quarter them, leaving peels on)
6 carrots, peeled and thickly sliced
4 stalks celery, sliced
3 T. cornstarch

Heat oil in Dutch oven or heavy pot; add the venison cubes and brown on all sides; sprinkle on salt and pepper while browning. Add the water, beef bouillon, Worcestershire sauce, and dry soup mix. Cover pot and simmer for 1½ hours.

Add the garlic, potatoes, carrots, and celery and continue to simmer until the vegetables are tender.

Remove ½ cup of the stew broth and mix in the cornstarch, stirring vigorously so it doesn't clump. Gradually pour the cornstarch mixture back into the stew, stirring constantly, and continue to simmer until the broth thickens.

Notes:

99 White Chicken Chili

2 tsp. oil
1 onion, chopped
2 T. cornstarch
4 cups chicken broth
2 cups cooked chicken, cut into bite-sized pieces
1 quart home-canned white beans (or 1-2 cans Great Northern
or white navy beans), drained
¼ tsp. garlic powder
2-4 tsp. cumin (start with 2 tsp. and add more if desired)
1 4-ounce can diced green chilies (mild or hot)
Monterey Jack cheese, shredded

Heat oil in a pot; add onion and sauté until pieces are translucent.

In a mixing bowl, stir together the cornstarch and broth. Gradually add it to the onion, stirring constantly while adding. Stir in all the other ingredients, except cheese, and bring to a boil. Reduce heat and simmer for 15 minutes.

Ladle into individual bowls and top with Monterey Jack cheese.

Notes:

A LITTLE SOMETHING EXTRA

I think a bowl of soup or stew isn't quite complete without a little something extra to go along with it. Time is a precious commodity, so if you're like me, you also don't want to have to fish through your cookbooks or recipe file to find that recipe for biscuits or cornbread—you want it handy. In the next few pages I'll share several basic recipes—things you can easily make to put the finishing touches to your delicious meal.

Biscuits

2 cups flour
4 tsp. baking powder
½ tsp. salt
5 T. vegetable shortening or lard
¾ cup milk

Preheat the oven to 450º.

In a medium mixing bowl, sift together the flour, baking powder, and salt. Cut the shortening into the flour mixture using a pastry blender or two butter knives, and continue until the mixture resembles coarse crumbles. Make a well in the center of the flour mixture and add the milk all at once. Stir with a fork until the dough leaves the sides of the bowl.

Now it's time to use your hands. Scoop up the ball of dough and turn it out onto a lightly floured surface; knead the dough about 10 times. Roll or pat out dough to ½-inch thickness; cut into biscuits using a floured biscuit cutter or a floured knife (who says that biscuits have to be round?). You can pat together the little pieces left from your first cuts to make as many biscuits as possible, but remember that the more you work the dough, the tougher the biscuits will be. Still, it's nice to use all the dough—even if the last one or two are misshapen. They will still taste good!

Place the biscuits on an ungreased cookie sheet and bake for 15-20 minutes, or until the biscuits are done and the tops are a light golden brown.

Note: For an even easier time of it, make drop biscuits instead of rolling out the dough and making cuts. All you need to do is increase the amount of milk to 1 cup, mix the dough, and then drop by overflowing tablespoonfuls onto a *greased* cookie sheet. Bake for 15-20 minutes. They won't look as pretty as the rolled version, but I hear no complaints when I do it that way.

A LITTLE SOMETHING EXTRA

Notes:

118

Cornbread

1 cup cornmeal
1 cup flour
¼ cup sugar
4 tsp. baking powder
½ tsp. salt
1 cup milk
1 egg, beaten
¼ cup vegetable oil

Preheat oven to 425°. Grease an 8 x 8-inch baking dish and set aside.

In a mixing bowl, stir together the cornmeal, flour, sugar, baking powder, and salt.

In another bowl, mix together the milk, egg, and vegetable oil; pour into the cornmeal mixture and stir just until ingredients are mixed.

Pour the batter into the prepared baking dish and bake for 20 minutes.

Note: I often decrease the sugar and add shredded Cheddar cheese and sometimes cooked bacon bits.

A LITTLE
SOMETHING EXTRA

Notes:

Popovers

If you have never had a popover, it's time you change that and try this recipe. You can make popovers in muffin tins, but we far prefer those little ovenproof Pyrex glass custard cups—one for each popover—which means 10 of the ½-cup custard cups. Although that is an expense, I maintain it's worth the money. We are rather addicted to them, which is odd considering there's not much to them. But there's just something about them.

1 cup flour
¼ tsp. salt (I usually go a little heavy on the salt)
1 tsp. sugar (optional) (We don't use sugar because we eat our
    popovers as a savory side to our meal, but it is cook's choice.)
1 T. butter, melted and cooled
1 cup milk
2 eggs

Preheat the oven to 375°. Grease or butter the custard cups or muffin tins.

In a mixing bowl, stir together the flour, salt, and sugar if you're using it. Mix thoroughly. Add the butter, milk, and eggs. Beat until the batter is very smooth, about 2½ minutes, and remember to scrape the sides often. My original recipe called for using electric beaters, but my Amish-made hand-cranked eggbeaters work well—and give me quite an upper arm workout!

Pour the batter into the prepared custard cups or muffin tins until they are about halfway full and bake on the center rack of your oven for 50-55 minutes.

Note: Like a soufflé, popovers wait for no one. When you bring them from the oven to the table, they will begin to deflate as they cool. So be prepared to have everyone at the table and ready to eat when the buzzer goes off.

Notes:

RECIPE INDEX

Soups

Amish Bean Soup   11

Barley Soup   12

Beef and Barley Soup   13

Beef and Green Bean Soup   14

Beefy Onion Rivel Soup   15

Boiled Potpie Soup   16

Cabbage and Apple Soup   17

Cabbage and Vegetable
    Chowder   18

Cabbage, Bean, and Ham
    Soup   19

Carrot and Sweet Potato Cream
    Soup   20

Celery Soup   21

Cheddar Cheese Soup with
    Pumpernickel Croutons   22

Cheeseburger Soup   23

Cheesy Onion Soup   24

Chicken Broth with Soda Cracker
    Dumplings   25

Chicken Chowder with
    Mushrooms   26

Chicken, Corn, and Noodle Soup
    27

Chicken Corn Chowder   28

Chili Bean Soup   29

Cold Fruit Soup   30

Corn and Clam Chowder   31

Corn and Tomato Chowder   32

Cottage Cheese and Vegetable
    Soup   33

Creamy Broccoli and Carrot
    Soup   34

Creamy Cabbage and Bacon
    Soup   35

Creamy Carrot and Rice
    Soup   36

Creamy Corn Chowder   37

Egg Soup   38

Farmer's Favorite Soup   39

Hamburger Soup   40

Leek and Potato Soup   41

Lentil Soup   42

Meat and Potatoes Soup with
   Hard-Boiled Eggs   43

Meatball Soup   44

Mock Oyster (Salsify) Soup   45

Old-Fashioned Chicken Noodle
   Soup   46

Old-Fashioned Vegetable Beef Soup
   47

Potato and Velveeta Cheese Soup
   48

Potato Rivel Soup   49

Potato Soup with Celery and Eggs
   51

Pumpkin Soup   52

Quick and Easy Tomato Soup   53

Spaghetti Soup   54

Split Pea Soup   55

Sweet Potato and Tortilla Chip
   Soup   56

Taco Soup   57

Turnip Soup   58

Vegetable Soup   59

White Bean Soup   60

Zucchini Soup   61

Stews

Apple Cider Pork Stew with Cheese
   Dumplings   65

Bean Stew   67

Beef and Sweet Potato Stew   69

Beef and Turnip Stew   70

Beef Stew with Coffee   71

Beef Stew with Dumplings   72

Black Beans with Pork and Citrus
   Sauce   73

Buffet Beef Cubes with
   Noodles   74

Chicken Alfredo Stew   75

Chicken and Lentil Stew   76

Chicken Goulash   77

Chicken Stew   78

Chicken, Sweet Potato, and
   Cabbage Stew   79

Chili Verde   80

Chili with Beans   81

Chili Without Beans   82

Chilly Day Stew   83

Classic Beef Stew   84

Colorful Beef Stew   85

Creamy Beef Stew   86

Creamy Chicken Stew   87

Creamy Potato and Vegetable
Stew   88

Easy Hamburger Stew   89

Elk Stew   90

Five-Hour Beef Stew   91

Gibson Stew   92

Ground Turkey Chili   93

I-Can't-Cook Stew   94

Just Pork Stew   94

Lamb Stew   96

Lentil and Sweet Potato
Stew   97

Lentil Stew   98

Lentil Stew with Ham and Swiss
Chard   99

Meatball Stew   100

No-Peek Stew   101

Old-Fashioned Oyster Stew   102

One-Dish Meal   103

Pot Roast with Carrots and
Potatoes   104

Quick and Easy Taco Stew   105

Rabbit Stew   106

Spicy Chicken Chili   107

Spicy Fish Stew   108

Squirrel Stew   109

Stonaflesch   110

Swiss Steak   111

Three-Bean Meatless Chili   112

Twenty-Four-Hour Beef Stew
113

Venison Stew   115

White Chicken Chili   116

A Little Something Extra

Biscuits   118

Cornbread   119

Popovers   120

99 Favorite Amish Recipes

Bring the Simple Life Home

The Amish are admired for their simple life, their intricate quilts, their forthright faith, and their homemade meals. Straight from the heart of Amish country, this new collection of hearty, wholesome recipes will remind you of the pleasures of the family table.

Learn to prepare easy and delicious dishes for your loved ones, including

- Caramel Apple Pie
- Farmer's Stew
- Shoofly Pie
- Haystack Supper
- Homemade Noodles

Find new favorites, make new traditions, and discover the pleasure of old-fashioned food!

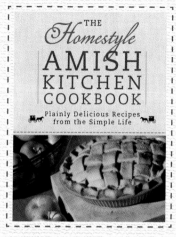

The Homestyle Amish Kitchen Cookbook

Let a Little Plain Cooking Warm Up Your Life

Who doesn't want simplicity in the kitchen?

Most of these delicious, easy-to-make dishes are simplicity itself. The Amish are a productive and busy people. They work hard in the home and on their farms, and they need good, filling food that doesn't require a lot of preparation and time. A few basic ingredients, some savory and sweet spices, and a little love make many of these meals a cook's delight. And if you want something a bit more complex and impressive, those recipes are here for you too.

Along with fascinating tidbits about the Amish way of life, you will find directions for lovely, old-fashioned foods, such as

- Scrapple
- Honey Oatmeal Bread
- Coffee Beef Stew
- Potato Rivel Soup
- Snitz and Knepp
- Shoofly Pie

Everything from breakfast to dessert is covered in this celebration of comfort food and family. Hundreds of irresistible options will help you bring the simple life to your own home and kitchen.

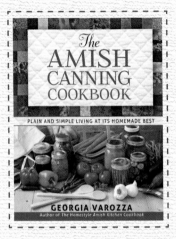

The Amish Canning Cookbook

Plain and Simple Living at Its Homemade Best

From the author of *The Homestyle Amish Kitchen Cookbook* comes a great new collection of recipes, hints, and Plain wisdom for everyone who loves the idea of preserving fresh, wholesome foods. Whether instructing a beginning canner or helping a seasoned cook hone her skills, certified Master Food Preserver Georgia Varozza shows people how to get the very best out of their food. Here, readers will find…

- a short history of canning
- lists of all the tools and supplies needed to get started
- basic instructions for safe canning
- recipes for canning fruit, vegetables, meat, soups, sauces, and more
- guidelines for adapting recipes to fit personal tastes

With its expert advice and warm tone, *The Amish Canning Cookbook* will become a beloved companion to those who love the tradition, frugality, and homestyle flavor of Amish cooking!

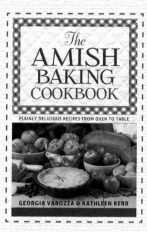

The Amish Baking Cookbook
Plainly Delicious Recipes from Oven to Table

Building on the success of *The Homestyle Amish Kitchen* (more than 60,000 copies sold), Georgia Varozza partners with experienced baker Kathleen Kerr to give you a cookbook filled with the foods most associated with the Plain and simple life: baked goods. This delicious collection of more than three hundred classic baking recipes for cookies, cakes, pies, bars, and breads will inspire you who love Amish fiction and are drawn to the Plain lifestyle to roll up your sleeves and start baking!

Whether you consider yourself a novice or a veteran in the kitchen, Georgia and Kathleen make it easy to make delicious baking recipes such as Amish Nut Balls and Brown Sugar Pie. Find the perfect recipe to prepare for that large weekend potluck, tonight's intimate family dinner, or a fun activity with the kids.

To learn more about Harvest House books and
to read sample chapters, visit our website:

www.harvesthousepublishers.com

HARVEST HOUSE PUBLISHERS
EUGENE, OREGON